"Headed Home is a tumultuous ride through the world of Major League Baseball. Glenn Wilson was an All Star, but he didn't really find his personal home plate until long after his last at bat. Glenn was always a funny, life-of-the-party type guy, but this book is more likely to produce the sweet sorrow of a tear."

Larry Dierker
Former player and manager
Houston Astros

"Glenn Wilson has bared his soul for all to read in Headed Home. His life as a baseball player has been well known, especially in the Houston area. But he has been willing to open up about his life off the field as well, giving us perspective on how many changes a person can undergo with God's guidance. From his relationships with his older brother, Johnie Jr., to his experiences with his coaches and managers, Glenn's honesty shines through. He leaves a powerful message for all to take from this book."

Bill Brown
Announcer of Houston Astros
Member of the Texas Sports Hall of Fame

HEADED HOME
A MLB All-star's Search for Truth

HEADED HOME
A MLB All-star's Search for Truth

BY

Glenn Wilson

With

Darrell Halk

LUCIDBOOKS

Headed Home

Published by Lucid Books in Brenham, TX.
www.LucidBooks.net

First Printing 2012

ISBN-13: 9781935909316
ISBN-10: 1935909312

Special Sales: Most Lucid Books titles are available in special quantity discounts. Custom imprinting or excerpting can also be done to fit special needs. Contact Lucid Books at info@lucidbooks.net.

Contents

Dedication

Glenn

This book is dedicated to my brother Johnie Wilson Jr. Johnie was asked by my Dad to take care of the family when he died. At the age of fourteen Johnie answered that call. Thank you for pushing me to be better. Without you I would have never made it. To my wife Kim, thank you for picking up where Johnie left off and making me a better man and standing by my side in the good and the bad times.

To book Glenn to speak at your next church, school or organization event please visit www.onbaseministries.com or email Glenn at glennwilson12@hotmail.com.

Darrell

This book is dedicated to my girls. Thank you to Tiffany for loving me in spite of my flaws. The life of a ministry family is never easy and you have walked with me and supported me like no one else could. Thank you for your work on this book in editing and structuring the first drafts of what would later become this powerful story. To my daughters Rylie and Macee, I am proud to be your daddy. Both of you are beautiful creations of God that make me smile every day.

Special thanks to Travis Gasper (editing), Vince Nauss, Larry Dierker, Bill Brown and Tiffany Halk for your contributions to this book.

To book Darrell to speak at your next church, school, organization event or to hire him for a writing project please visit www.norkbook.com.

Chapter 1

"Shit house or castle, kid. Shit house or castle."
These were the last words I would hear before stepping into the batter's box on July 16, 1985 at the Major League Baseball All-Star game held in the Minneapolis, Minnesota Metrodome. I was called on to pinch hit for the pitcher Jeff Reardon in the top of the ninth inning. The bases were loaded (Jack Clark on third, Willie McGee on second and Tim Wallach at first), we had two outs

and the opposing pitcher was Willie Hernandez. Willie, also known during his career by his Spanish name Guillermo, was the player I was traded for before the 1984 season. Hernandez not only led my former team to the World Series, which they would win to become world champions; he also won the Cy Young award, MVP of the American League and the Sporting News Pitcher of the year in 1984. (Baseball Reference)

While Hernandez was achieving great accolades in 1984, I was stinking up the National League, eventually becoming a part-time player for my new team, the Philadelphia Phillies. Those words ringing in my ears, "Shithouse or castle," were being screamed at me by the guy who would accumulate more hits than anyone in major league baseball history: Pete Rose.

To say it took great effort to remain calm would be an understatement. Here was the legend, Pete Rose, the most intense baseball player I would ever encounter, calling me out. This was my time to shine, my one chance to prove to the Tigers brass that they were wrong for letting their number one draft pick in 1980 get away. I had suffered so much anguish since that trade, and no one knew it but me. I wanted them to feel the regret I felt in being dealt when they saw me defeat Hernandez head to head.

I guess I should have been proud of the fact that I had made an all-star team, but pain and discomfort is what I felt. When I was traded from Detroit to Philadelphia, in some ways I was relieved because the rumors of me being trade bait had started circulating back at the end of the '83 season and continued all the way through the winter and into spring training. So as much as it hurt, I also felt some relief that this circus was over. Another relief was getting away from Sparky Anderson. This move brought sheer joy because Sparky never liked me and the feeling was mutual. The awful year I had in 1984 for the Phillies was capped off with me watching the Tigers win the World Series as I was back in St. Petersburg, Florida attending instructional league. The instructional league is where organizations send their top prospects for extra work for the duration of about 6 weeks.

I must admit that I cried watching the Tigers win it all. I never pulled so hard for the Padres in all my life. After watching my former teammates celebrate in their clubhouse on the television, I walked outside disgusted and actually took a look over the balcony of the 120 floor complex my wife Kim and I were staying at, and I remember thinking that would do the trick. I could end it all now, and not have to answer the questions of how I felt about the Tigers winning it all. It was a quick thought and for that I am thankful. Now it was time to get serious about being in the best shape of my life and ready to become the player I had been my rookie year for those Tigers, except now for the Phillies.

As I stepped up to the plate at the All-Star game just one and a half years after this trade, Vin Scully announced me to the TV audience saying, "And now the trade for the entire world to see."

The world watched and with the bases loaded in the top of the ninth I am about to dig in. Could this be my defining moment? Is this the pinnacle of my success? How will I be remembered? These things ran through my mind as I stood in to face Hernandez.

We will come back to this moment, but first I will try to help you understand the Glenn Wilson that made it to Big Leagues in less than two years after being a number one draft pick. I was the eighteenth person selected overall in ,1980; this was the year that Darryl Strawberry was the number one overall pick.

To define me, we must look at where this journey began. I grew up in a very small suburb of Houston, Texas, called Channelview. My father died of a heart attack when I was six years old. My mom had a mountain to climb when she lost my dad, because she had just lost her husband, had three sons to raise, and had never held a job outside of the home. She had been an athlete in her native state of Mississippi, so I guess she found her strength through athletics. My mom was not a coddler of her boys. She loved us but was a foul-mouthed, in your face, get it done or else type of person. She eventually found a job working for Metropolitan Insurance, but she never brought her work home with her. She made time to cook two meals a day and make our sack lunches for school. She smoked Winston 100s and went through two or three packs a day. She was the typical mom: she would clean the house, make sure we brushed our teeth and that we got into bed on time. At the time of Dad's death, Johnie Jr. was fourteen years old, Edward Roe was eleven, and I was six. Mom was strong, but life had dealt her a pretty tough challenge.

Johnie Wilson Sr. was only forty-one years old when death called his name. I was too young to have any distinct memories of him. I never grieved his death until 1990 when I was thirty years old and saw the movie *Field of Dreams*. Thank you Kevin Costner. It was then I realized all that had been missed with his early death. What a powerful line in the movie when Ray Kinsella says, "Hey Dad… Wanna have a catch?" It was this quote that moved me, as I am sure it did many men watching this movie.

Johnie Jr. grew up the day that Dad died, and he took on his shoulders the obligation of protecting and watching over the rest of us. Before Dad's death, Johnie had been the best baseball player Channelview had ever seen and I was told Dad loved bragging about him. He could hit mammoth home runs at the age of twelve. He loved baseball and Mickey Mantle. He watched the "NBC Game of the Week" every Saturday on our TV. He taught himself to hit by watching those games and emulating the stances and skills of the players.

My middle brother, Roe played baseball as well, but I don't think it was something he loved. To say we were poor would be accurate, but I never knew it. Being the youngest of three boys, I was fighting for attention and love. Johnie was the hero in this house at the time, and I was chasing and coveting his attention

For some reason, after Dad's passing Mom quit taking us to church. It could have been for a variety of reasons;

maybe she was tired now that she was working and trying to raise three boys, or maybe she was mad at God. I never knew for sure. She was foul-mouthed and a little racist when I was young, but I saw her grow out of these habits. She and my dad had grown up in Southern Mississippi where racism was still a way of life. The town of Channelview where I grew up had no black residents, and it was not until high school, through athletics, that I would encounter someone of another color.

Johnie was very serious about making it to the Big Leagues, and I would become his training tool. I did not mind because at that time in history there were no video games, not even Pong. Johnie was eight years older than me, but since he had to practice he decided I would play plastic baseball with him in our backyard. With his love of the game as inspiration, he had turned our backyard into a small replica of Boston's Fenway Park. He used chicken wire to erect a twenty-foot tall left field wall that he even spray-painted green. Even though he was eight years my senior, he realized I could compete with him by the time I was six. Not wanting to play was not a valid option to Johnie as he would hold my head to the ground until I agreed to participate. Little did I know that Johnie's pushing me to play would be what refined my athletic talent and helped prepare me for a career in baseball. My big brother's in your face attitude and pushing for perfection would also leave an imprint on me. He was the only male figure I had to look up to in my life.

In those days, the hardware store sold twenty plastic golf balls for seventy-five cents. They were made of a really hard, dense plastic and if one got away from the pitcher, it left a welt. You could hit those balls for three months before they would start to crack. We played a game Johnie invented called "Automatic Men." Since there were only two of us, Johnie would decide if a ground ball in the hole between short and third was a hit or a great play by the imaginary shortstop. After awhile of playing by the rules I started to realize his defense was better than mine.

Johnie hated losing. As I grew older, I started to complain and quit in order to get my way, but that just led to more of my head being held down in the ground until I started to play again. Johnie did give me one advantage by breaking our broom stick to the size of a 28 inch bat for me to use as my hitting tool. The down side of this "bat" was that when mom asked where her broom was, of course I got blamed for it being broken.

Johnie was also an intimidator, his anger as quick as Carl Lewis running the 100-meter dash. When I started to hit his famous knuckle curveball over the monster chicken wire wall in left, you could bet I was getting one of those welts courtesy of a Johnie Wilson fastball to the ribs on the next pitch. Johnie was 5"10 by the time he was 12, so it was in my best interest to do what he said when Mom was not around, if I had any desire to live another day.

I played plastic ball even after Johnie moved out. I played with my friends Doug Cooper, Richard Hanson (who I fought one day because he did not want to play),Dana Wilson, Russell Owens, Kelly and Mark Smith, Joe Khoury (whose mom and dad CJ and Lenda are like mine now) and Cary and Randy Cleveland, who were my closest friends all the way up to the age of sixteen. I did not realize plastic baseball was going to be my ticket to the major leagues.

To say Johnie was tough on me would not be telling the whole truth. He was the meanest older brother you could have. I still have visions of this giant of a man screaming at me if I made an error or if, God forbid, I struck out. He yelled at me, called me names, and did not care who was around. I had to be perfect, and we all know no one is perfect. I will never forget when I made an error at shortstop one night when I was ten and he was eighteen. I was coming to the dugout after the inning ended and he was screaming at me, "Lift your head up! If you make an error, lift it up! Lift it up!"

I finally yelled back, "Shut up!"

"What are you going to do about it?"

I went in the dugout and grabbed my helmet and bat, and when I came out to the on-deck circle he was still yelling as I was headed to home plate.

"Why don't you hit a home run then?"

"I will, now SHUT…UP!"

Low and behold I became the first Channelview ten-year-old to hit a home run. It felt like I was floating around the bases. After touching home I went to the fence and shouted at Johnie, "WELL, I DID IT!"

My Mom turned to Johnie to see his response and knew I did not enjoy that moment one bit. Johnie's response was, "Well…he was right. He did it."

When he saw how I was being taught the game by coaches at the ages of ten, eleven, and twelve, and since he was out of high school and working now, Johnie decided to start coaching in Senior League Baseball. He took on the worst team in Senior League, while I was still in Little League. He started to build this team around me before I even got up there. When I was old enough to join his team, we were set. We went thirty-seven and three in my three years of Senior League and by our second year, since we were winning nearly every game, there were so many people at our games they had to park a mile away. They were really there to see us lose as we became almost hated for our propensity to win.

Johnie was definitely your typical older brother, meaning that we fought. When I say we fought, it was always verbal, at times it got a little physical, but he never abused me. I know he pushed me so hard because he wanted me to be the best, like most dads hope for their kids. I was definitely scared of him, because I had seen him when he was angry with someone outside our family, and I never wanted to see that side of him directed at me. I saw him beat a guy half to death for almost hitting his new car. I said ALMOST hitting his car.

Later in life I would not want to be around him because, honestly, I was sick of him. He made me stay later than the other players, and even when I got to high school ball, he would show up with his fungo bat and say, "Let's get it on." I did not want to, but I had no choice. His dream of becoming a "Big Leaguer" had already died, and I became his mission. "Operation Get Glenn to the Majors" was in full swing. I was going to live his dream for him, just like so many dads today push their sons to live their broken dreams. You bet he made me better than everyone, but he also made me want to relocate to a different area code. Now, maybe he is the reason I became a pro baseball player, but the way he went about it was worse than any parent I have ever seen. What made it even harder was that Mom would support him and back him up while all I wanted was to feel loved.

One day in the eighth grade, while sitting on the steps outside the junior high basketball gym waiting on my Mom to pick me up, I asked one of our coaches if a freshman had ever made the varsity baseball team. His response was, "No, and don't think you will either."

I thought, "You SOB, I will show you."

For some reason if you told me I could not do something, I would make it my goal to prove you wrong. I did make the Varsity team as a freshman and 1st team all district. I would also play football, basketball, and pole vault, long jump and high jump for the track team. In basketball I had great form on my shot, but I was a terrible shooter. I just could not make the ball go through the hoop, unless it was a lay-up. Freshman and sophomore years were exciting, but you had to deal with the older guys and the peer pressure that comes with the jump to high school. I never drank or used drugs for various reasons, and I had a job at a gas station and a couple of girls I liked, so that helped me keep busy and out of trouble.

I received a call from a pro scout named Lenny Yochim the summer after my junior year. He said they were having a tryout in a neighboring town and wanted to see me play in a game that day. So I showed up, in spite of the fact I had a fever of one-hundred-two Fahrenheit. After the scrimmage started, it was clear that they were looking very closely at a pitcher who was from North Shore High School. During the game, I went four for four hitting this guy who was not in the best shape. The scout asked me to get on the mound and I pitched three innings of no-hit ball, striking out four.

Later that same summer, the Pirates were coming to Houston and the scout called my house and invited my mother and me (along with a guest) to come see the Pirates play the Astros. So I took Gary Ellison along since he was one of the funniest humans on the planet. I remember having seats right behind the on-deck circle, about three rows up, and John Candelaria was pitching. The week before Candelaria had pitched a no hitter, so we were excited. As we were watching the game, the scout and another man came and sat with us. The scout introduced the other man as Joe Brown. Back then I did not know any front office people or what their titles meant, but I later found out that Mr. Brown was the Pirates' general manager. He told us that they were going to draft me in the upcoming June draft.

Then I opened my big mouth and said, "Don't I have to graduate high school first?"

He asked, "What? You haven't graduated yet?"

"No sir, I'm just a junior."

He disappeared in a hurry and so did the scout who had brought me to the game. I never heard from them again. I still don't understand to this day is why didn't he come back after my senior year. I had an even better year as a senior.

Even though I was not drafted out of high school for pro ball, I did get an offer from Sam Houston State University to play football. That was fine with me. Then John Skeeters, who was the baseball coach for Sam Houston State, saw me while attending a Cincinnati Reds tryout camp before spring football all started.

He asked, "Are you the kid from Channelview coming to play football?"

"Yes sir."

"Do want to play baseball, too?"

"Will it get me out of spring football?"

"Yes."

So of course I said, "Sure, I'll play."

This coach and I were never close, and we had a huge run-in towards the end of my junior year in college. He was the kind of coach that nobody connected with and frankly no one liked. I played football only one year at SHSU and made all conference as a punter. I also split time as a receiver, scoring two touchdowns.

Starting my sophomore year, we had a new football coach who only used me as a punter. It drove me nuts to stand around all game and then go punt. After the second game of the season, I was called to the head coach's office. It seemed that while I was at summer school taking History Two, I should have been taking History One, since I had failed it. They informed me I was ineligible for my scholarship. Since Coach Skeeters was my advisor and I was now out of a scholarship, I went looking for him to dish out a piece of my mind. I found him at the grocery store in town, and he informed me that if I could come up with seven hundred dollars, then I could be on just a baseball scholarship.

Whether he did it on purpose or not makes no difference, but I believe he knew that I could make a bigger impact in baseball over football. I went home that winter, got a job, and made the money, and I was ready to have my first full year of year-round baseball.

I broke a lot of the records at Sam Houston State during my sophomore year and had become even more confident. I had always what everyone else called cocky, but I saw it as confidence. I was little when Joe Namath came along with the Jets in Super Bowl III, and he became my first hero with Muhammad Ali running a close second. I don't know why but I loved their confidence. I respected the guys that talked a little smack, believed in themselves and backed it up. They gave me desire to be like them. I wanted to emulate them on and off the field. I would end up paying a dear price for this attitude.

During the second game of a double hitter my junior year against Lamar University, there were runners at first and second with two outs in the seventh inning. We were down by a run. In doubleheaders in college, you only played seven innings, so this was the last inning of the game. In game one that day I had hit a home run in the same situation on a three and one count that won the game. This time I would ground out into a game ending double play.

During our team gathering after the game, our coach said that I was suspended for the final three games.

"Why?"

"You know why."

"No, I don't know why." All my teammates were looking at me like I did know why.

I shouted, "Why?"

"You saw me give you the take sign."

"No you didn't."

"That's the end of this discussion. And while suspended, you'll watch the final three games from the stands."

I shouted, "The hell I will! And you did not put the take sign on! If I am suspended, I quit!"

I kicked my shoes off, grabbed my glove, and walked home to my apartment. I proceeded to punch a hole in my door, and to my surprise, my mother was standing in my apartment. I told her what had happened. She said, "Son, the draft is two weeks away and if you quit, what will the pro teams think of you?"

To this day, and until they bury me, I will say I never saw a take sign. The coach to this day will tell you I ignored the sign. Let's think about this for a second; I had tied my school home run record with that home run in the first game and was hitting .439 for the season. What coach, in their right mind, would put a take sign on with a three and one count to one of the nation's top hitters? I swallowed my pride that day, went back to the field, and asked the coach to let me back on the team. He said yes, but I would also have to apologize to the team.

The team played those last three games and they hit somewhere around ten home runs, all of them with me sitting in the stands. With the draft coming up and the playoffs starting, and since my least favorite person was our coach, I could have cared less about winning those games. I only wanted the season to be over so I could finally get away from him. I learned so much from this situation, that I would be able to use later in life when I became a manager. Never have any of your players or your bench players think you're not in their corner, and never show a player up in front of his teammates. John could have handled this situation better; where I would have worked hard and done whatever he asked of me. Instead, I would not have the least bit of sympathy for him when he was finally fired. Although today I can proudly say he is a dear friend.

Chapter 2

It is funny how we have all these plans for our life and they never work out how we imagine. I was going to play in the NFL, not the MLB. After three years of college, a .439 batting average my junior year, tying the schools home run record, and breaking my RBI record, the Major League Baseball June Draft was about to change my life.

Up until then I had never given much thought to anything really, except to be a pro athlete and have a family. I had a life to live, places to go, and people to meet. My only priority was to live for myself and my goals. I did not even go to classes during my junior year after I started hearing the rumors of being a high draft pick. Not like it would have mattered. The only classes I attended in those three years were solely for the purpose of staying eligible. Pro baseball was about to fulfill my dream of being a pro athlete, and at that point in my life nothing else mattered.

The draft was one of the most exciting days of my life. My mother, Roe, Johnie and his wife Diane and their son Johnie Wilson the 3rd, my fiancée Kim and my best buddy Randy Cleveland all came over that June morning to wait by the phone with me. Back then, there was no ESPN, so that meant no networks were hosting the draft live on television, and there were no home computers to check out the draft details, so all draft notifications came via telephone. At 10 A.M. the phone rang and there was an older man on the other end of the line.

"Is this Glenn Wilson?" he asked.

"Yes sir."

"This is Hoot Evers and I am with the Detroit Tigers. We just made you our number one pick." Hearing that absolutely filled me with so much joy I felt I could jump through the roof.

"Ok," was all I could say in return.

He said he would be coming down from New York in a couple of days to offer me a contract. I thought Johnie was going to bust through the roof with me. He had all the magazines and was telling me who their former first round picks were and all sorts of information about their organization. Man, I did not care. I had done it! I was seeing my dream come true! My mom, who always smiled anyways, was grinning from ear to ear. Everyone was so excited. There was a TV station and a newspaper coming by to interview me. It was awesome. Johnie said their manager was Sparky Anderson. I remember thinking, "Wow! The guy that led the Big Red Machine was going to be my manager."

Those next two days were like walking on a cloud. Friends and family were calling to congratulate me and my family. Johnie and I started discussing how to negotiate the signing bonus, though neither of us had ever done such a thing. We decided at the last minute to turn the air conditioner off and tell Mr. Evers that it was not working. If you have ever been to Houston in the summer time, you know it can get pretty hot and humid there. We had a window unit, and when it was turned off, it became scorching hot. Johnie had also researched the signing bonuses that the last two number one picks of the Tigers had received. They were Kirk Gibson and Rick Leach. For the first time in my life, I was thinking of things I could buy. I was also about to find out what large sums of money can do to a person. More importantly, I was about to get an education in negotiating, which was something I had never done. This would be one of the areas I wish I had thought about when I was dreaming of being a pro athlete.

A week later Hoot arrived right on time. He must have been really comfortable when he came in because his first offer pissed Johnie off.

"What were you thinking?" Hoot asked first.

"The same as what Gibson and Leach got," I said.

"You are no Gibson."

"What were you thinking?" Johnie asked.

"We are prepared to offer around $40,000."

The offer made me mad. "I'm worth a hundred."

"No."

Then Johnie spoke up. "What about fifty?" I turned and glared at Johnie.

"What are you doing? This is not your life. It's mine."

Then it was on, as, Johnie and I started a minor, in-your-face, screaming match. Hoot said he would go to a pay phone and call Detroit to see what he could do. We did not even know he left we were so involved in our conversation.

I was a man now. No, I was the man now, and Johnie Wilson Jr. was not going to run my life. Once Johnie left with squealing tires, I contacted the Hendricks brothers, who Stan Blinka of the New York Jets, a former linebacker and teammate at SHSU, had recommended to me. I told them I wanted their representation, and I also mentioned that I was pretty sure I would be their first client that was a first round pick in baseball. They asked where we were in the negotiations, I told them and Evers' offer, and then they said they would take it from there. Since they did not charge anything until after you had one full year in the big leagues, I thought having an agent was so cool. They even completed your taxes and investments for you, if you wanted. When it was all said and done, the Hendricks team was able to secure me $22,500 more than Mr. Evers had originally offered me, which put the grand total of my bonus at $62,500.

Although I wanted the money, it was not what was most on my mind at the time. I just wanted to begin being a pro, a grown man getting paid to play a kids' game. The hard part about having new found money was the fact that my friends and family started putting their hands out.

Tigers' farm director, the late Bill Lajoie, would send me straight to Double A right out of college. The farm director's job was to evaluate a minor leaguer's talent level and help them develop into major league talent. Lajoie believed in pushing prospects, and it seemed he also believed in me.

The minor leagues were enjoyable. Once again, I did not make many friends because I did not think I would be with any of those guys very long. I was right.

I never really thought about the Big Leagues up to that point, but I knew I would get there eventually. I had breezed through Double A, making the transition from third base to the outfield look extremely easy. They transitioned me into the outfield, because in my first year of Minor League ball playing third, I made thirty-three errors in only seventy-seven games. That is not easy to do, and even if I did happen to catch it, I would throw it away. It was the first time in my life I had lost confidence in anything other than shooting a basketball.

During my second year in Double A, I experienced a dreadful slump at the plate. Then I saw a special on the television about Pete Rose one Sunday night. I do not remember what they were talking about because I was studying his swing. I came to the park the next day with my Pete Rose approach and stance. I went on a nineteen-game hitting streak with two or more hits. My average went from .240 to .300 during this period. They put me in centerfield, and I had a great year both offensively and defensively.

The Minors really are fun when you are first coming up. You do not mind the thirteen-hour bus rides, the leave-the-light-on-for-you motels. I was in the southern league right after the movie Urban Cowboy came out, so the bars on the road were hopping. The rest of the Minor League routine is just like what they do in the Big Leagues. This is to prepare you for how it is in The Show.

Being a first round pick does have some draw backs. One of those drawbacks is that other guys know you received a large signing bonus and the organization is going to keep you around longer because of the money invested in you. Not many guys ever showed much animosity towards me, but I was the butt of several jokes. It did not bother me, because I knew where I was headed... and where they probably would not be going.

During this season, I also learned that pitchers threw at you on purpose and obviously, I was green to the inside part of the game. I only charged the mound one time in the Minors because a pitcher threw at me. It was the son of a Major League manager that I would have later in my career. No one really won the fight; most baseball fights never have a winner. I used to think that if a hitter charged the mound, the rest of the players should have to form a ring and not be allowed to join in. Now *that* would bring more fans out to the games.

When I was called up to Triple A, towards the end of the '81 season, my manager was Jim Leyland. My Triple A team, the Evansville Triplets, would make the playoffs but be eliminated early.

In 1982, I went to my first Big League spring training and the fans really did not have an idea who I was. When you get to your first Big League camp, you see all the well-known players being asked for autographs. When I walked by, I could hear people asking, "Who is the guy wearing number sixty-eight?" This experience was humility at its best. I longed for the day when people would want my autograph. That day would come sooner than later.

I did not make the big club after spring training, so I was sent back to Triple A to begin my season with the Evansville Tigers. I would not stay there long as I was called up after our very first game of the season. It goes without saying that being called up to The Show was a defining moment of my life. I was finally living out the day I always knew would come.

In the opening day game at Triple A Evansville in 1982, I hit two home runs and was pumped about my performance. As I was coming off the field, there was Lajoie on the top step of the dugout. When I got to him, he stopped me and whispered, "They need you in The Show. Do not act excited when you go into the clubhouse." They had some injuries in the outfield on the Big Club, and they were calling Howard Johnson and me up to Detroit. We had to catch a flight at seven the next morning.

I have no idea how I was able to remain calm. Some of the other players came up to me and told me good luck. Others said, "See you back here in a little while." When I got to my truck, my wife screamed at the top of her lungs. Her yell was so deafening that I thought surely there was a snake in the truck. It scared me so bad I yelled, "What is it?"

She said, "We're going to the Big Leagues!"

The Big Leagues. Wow, I was going to the Big Leagues. Today the sport looks very different, with games on anywhere in the world. Back in 1982, most games were just regional coverage along with the NBC Game of the Week. They had also recently added Monday Night Baseball with the late Howard Cossell, who I thought was awesome.

Before I even started with the Big Leagues, I had to pack my apartment; I finally finished around three in the morning. I caught three hours of sleep and headed to the airport, while my wife drove our truck to Detroit. Little did I know my childhood friends Randy Cleveland and Dan Kirby were riding a bus from Channelview to Detroit, just to see me play.

Our first stop, after taking the shuttle bumper out of Evansville, was Indianapolis. After flying through a thunderstorm in a twelve-seat prop plane, getting on a jet was nice. Then it was on to Toronto to meet the Big Club. Walking into that clubhouse for the first time and seeing my last name on a big league jersey with my hero's number 12, hanging in a Big League locker, is as good as it gets. I just stood there and stared. Suiting up and just taking batting practice in a Big League stadium was unbelievable. Never in my career was I more happy that I did not play in the game because that night I was just soaking it all in. Besides, the game was in Toronto, and I did not really want my first Big League at-bat to come in another country...that would just not be American.

The next day's game would be the home opener in Detroit. They had been snowed-out of their first home series and opened their season on the road. In Detroit, opening day has a playoff atmosphere with a packed house and the weather a wintery thirty degrees. I can still remember walking down the tunnel to the field, and the strangest part was that I was not feeling overwhelmed. I could hear the loud speakers playing the theme from *Chariots of Fire* and I remembered Ty Cobb had played on that field. I knew without a doubt this field is where great things were going to happen for me. That was pretty bold thinking for a twenty-three year old kid. I had never lacked confidence. I felt I had been preparing for this my whole life.

Back in my day, no one prepared you for dealing with the media in the Big Leagues, so I was very green. It wasn't until players became a target for the paparazzi that teams started bringing in media coaches. Back then, writers and reporters wanted to be your friend and were not looking to bury a guy to earn a promotion. Some would go tell your manager what you were doing or saying, but that was about it. When Steve

Carlton stopped talking to the media because a writer talked about what he is doing off the field or about his wife, then the gloves came off back in those days. I see why players are so private now, if they are caught on tape doing anything, it could end up on You Tube, TMZ, or ESPN. You never know when a recorder is on, capturing life's events.

I am glad I did not play in today's era, except for the dollars that are being paid. Look how hard they came down on the steroid players when the entire baseball world knew tons of the players were on them. The owners knew, but the fans were packing the parks to see those home runs, which meant more money for owners. I wanted to see Barry Bonds at the plate as much as anybody. Now the writers are saying that any player that did steroids doesn't get their vote for the Hall of Fame. In my opinion, there were not many players from '93 to '07 that were not using something (pitchers included). There should be a wing in the Hall of Fame called "During the Steroid Era." I'm not going to name any names, but there are some guys saying to themselves, "I can't believe I did not get caught."

After my first two weeks in The Show, I was hitting close to .400 and had made some really outstanding defensive plays. It was after this performance that I got my first taste of MLB media. A reporter, with a camera rolling, asked me if I was surprised at how well I was playing, since it was my first time being in the Big Leagues. My response was, "I'm not surprised, but I bet the fans are pretty surprised. I've been doing these things my whole life; you guys just haven't been there to see it."

That comment would not go over well with some of my teammates, and especially with Sparky. I was just speaking the truth, but as I would learn later, you are supposed to be humble. I still believe if you have any doubts about what you are doing, then you probably should not be doing it.

A lot of people thought I was cocky, but I did not care; I was just always good at baseball. That first game in Detroit, I was called on to pinch hit. I took four pitches; three of them were called strikes. When I got back to the bench, our hitting coach, Gates Brown, said to me, "I can hear the fans now, kid, saying the boy sure looks good when he takes. I wonder how he looks when he swings." I busted out laughing.

I was only around Gates Brown for two years, but he gave me a piece of advice I have never forgotten. He told me one afternoon game when I was not in the lineup, "Don't worry about the things you can't control." We developed a good relationship. We had some fun, like in Anaheim when Reggie Jackson had gone to them as a free agent and was complaining about how he was not making the money he thought he deserved. So when Reggie would hit a home run, the fans would throw change on the field for him. I just could not resist picking up the money that Reggie did not get in his half-inning. I would come back to the dugout with a pocket full of change and Gates would count it. Then, when Reggie came up to bat, we pulled for him to hit a home run. Gates would say, "Ok kid, time to go to work. We only need seventy-five more cents for a pack of cigarettes." I respected him as much as anyone I would ever meet in baseball. He was the first player ever signed out of prison. We also had a flight out of Toronto one late evening and back then the Tigers were still flying commercial. The plane we were on was not a jet, but it was a propeller plane. Like me, some of the older players did not like flying. After we were seated, the pilot came on the speaker and said that we would have to wait about an hour until takeoff while they worked on the fuel line. Now I am not a mechanic, but when some of those older players heard this, they got up and went and found their own flights. I looked at Gates sitting beside me, and since I was a rookie, he said "Don't even think about it." He knew I wanted to get off the plane too, but I guess there are some things in life as a rookie you just have to ride out.

The next night I would get my first Big League start and my first hit. The hit would be a double to the left-center gap. The pitcher was Ron Guidry, and as I was standing on second base, he turned to me and nodded his head. I thought he was a first class guy. I hit a double off of the "Louisiana Lightening" and he showed me some respect.

The rest of that season was not good from a team aspect, but it was great for me. I fell in love with being a Big Leaguer and everything that went with it. I enjoyed having people cheer for me and wanting my autograph. I finished the 1982 season hitting .292 with twelve home runs, playing mostly center and right field. I also found out, while in Yankee Stadium, that I was going to be a father for the first time. There were some cover stories in the newspapers, and writers wanted to talk to me on a regular basis. I was falling in love with all the attention.

I also had a very frightful thing happen in New York. After a night when I had hit a two-run homer off Goose Gossage, while the reporters were gathered in front of my locker asking me questions, Howard Johnson walked by and said Gossage throws more like a turkey. The next day, after ordering room service, a newspaper headline in the sports section said, "Goose Throws More like Turkey than Goose," a quote attributed to me.

I nearly choked on my lunch as this misquote petrified me and made me furious. I gave the sportswriter, Mike McAlary, a wake-up call from the lobby that morning to let him know I was not happy about being misquoted and that I planned to kill him. I also let McAlary know he had just assured my decapitation. (McAlary, 1998)

I left for the ballpark early to get a note to Gossage by way of one of the clubhouse kids, letting him know it was a misquotation. He never responded, and I became even more worried, thinking that the next time I faced him I would be dead. So when I saw him walking to the bullpen right before the game, I started running to loosen up. I timed it so I could tell him to his face that I did not say what the paper had reported. He responded by saying, "Don't worry about it. That's how the media is in New York." I started to feel relieved, until he continued, "But I still have to knock you on your ass the next time I face you."

I would face him in Detroit the next week, and he did knock me down with the first pitch he threw to me. I then proceeded to hit a double off the wall on his next pitch. Gossage was the type of pitcher that could silence a crowd when he started warming up. He did not blow saves and the fans felt the game was over if the Yankees had a lead going into the seventh. This story about Gossage would be told to me many times by my future pitching coach in Pittsburgh, Ray Miller. It became comical, because Ray would tell this story about how you could hear a pin drop in the stadium when Gossage would start to warm up in the bullpen.

At the end of that year, I was awarded the Tiger Rookie of the Year award.

That winter, since Kim and I were going to be parents, we decided to stay in Detroit to make money by signing autographs. My first year's salary was the minimum of $33,000. So we rented Lance and Arlyne Parrish's townhouse to live in, and on December 16th we had our first of three sons. This would be the first time I felt the presence of God. Glenn Wilson, Jr. had come into this world on the day after a huge snow storm blew into Detroit. As we were driving to the hospital at three in the morning, it was snowing hard. Being from Texas, I had never driven in snow. While driving to Ypsilanti, I was stopped by an officer. He tried to say something, but I cut him off and said we were about to have a baby. He said, "Hey, you're Glenn Wilson." That would be the first of many times I would be recognized as being a major league ballplayer in public. He asked what hospital we were heading to and said to follow him.

Life was good. I was about to turn twenty-four, I had a wife and a son, and I was living my dream. The Tigers gave me a raise to $70,000 that winter, and I would be heading to Lakcland, Florida for my first spring training as an established Big Leaguer. That meant people would know me and want my autograph. It was so cool getting off a bus or walking into a stadium with people screaming your name, asking for an autograph. There are stages you go through as a ball player, and when fans first want your autograph, you love it. It was an honor for me to sign for my fans, but after two years of it, you try to avoid signing. Then when you become an All-Star, you can tell people no. I remember seeing Gibson scream, "No!" at people. I think he was doing it to be funny, but it wasn't. I remember my first autograph signing when a woman around forty was so nervous she was shaking. I thought that the power we had as ballplayers was amazing. Growing up, I was never an autograph collector or a fan of a team.

I felt the '83 season was a good one for me, but from the media articles where Sparky was quoted about me, it was obvious he was not pleased. I remember one incident when we went to Texas to play the Rangers. Sparky knew I would have family there, and some pitchers on our team had been complaining about the fact that I was making too many unnecessary diving catches on fly balls. Even though it could appear that way, I just felt more comfortable sliding on balls in front of me. I never made a catch to make it appear spectacular, but I could not convince Sparky of this truth. I tried to convince him of his error in a meeting we had with Roger Craig and Alex Grammas before the Texas series. In an attempt to defend myself, I told all of them in a stern manner that they did not know what they were talking about.

I found myself riding the pine and not in the starting lineup that night, but I was called on in the bottom of the ninth inning to replace Gibson in right field for defensive purposes. Then, with a one run lead, a runner at second, and two outs, a sharp line drive was hit to my left. As I was running for the ball, I realized I would not catch it without diving. This was so ironic and uncomfortable because as I was running I was thinking about the meeting earlier that day. Thank God I dove or the game would have been tied. As I was coming off the field to the congratulations, there was Sparky. He said nothing, but I had to give him a little grin, as if to say, "leave me alone and let me play." What was the big deal? As long as the ball was caught, who cares how you do it?

In my mind, the remainder of the 1983 season was decent. My average ended up at .265, and even though I was hitting at different spots all over the lineup, I was able to drive in sixty-five runs. Bill Lajoie commented in his book that he felt I was never the same player because of a brush-back pitch he had seen me take during the 1983 season. My guess is that he meant I was now scared of the ball; well, in this case Bill was wrong. Do not get me wrong, I completely respected Bill Lajoie as a person and a baseball man. When I was called up to the Big Leagues for the very first time, he was the man to tell me, and he went out of his way to help my wife get settled in Detroit (Anup Sinha, 2010).

Toward the end of '83, the rumors started that I might be traded. Back then, sports writers formed close relationships with some of the players and loved talking about what they had heard through the rumor mill. I personally hated all the rumors because I did not want to be traded, but I also could not stand Sparky. I wanted to play twenty years in Detroit and be their mainstay in right field during those years. In my opinion Sparky had an ego bigger than Texas and wanted everyone to know that he was the man. Since I had an even bigger ego, and I was the one playing the game, it was probably the best thing to trade me. I was sure Sparky and I would clash in a bad way at some point.

All winter, I was rumored to be going here or there, and it never stopped. But then it grew interesting. I was told to bring a third base-man's glove to spring training because I would be competing for the third base job. After taking ground balls every day before spring games started, I started the first spring training game at third. This was a position I had not played since being drafted and sent to Double A, where I made thirty-three errors in just half a season. I had no idea why anyone thought I could play third, unless they were trying to trade a guy.

In that first game on a ground ball hit to me, with a runner at first, I did not get the ball out of my glove as fast as I should have. We still turned the double play, but the next morning the papers quoted Sparky ripping me on my performance. Sparky was saying that I nearly got Whitaker killed and that the third base experiment was over. I did not think it made a lot of sense in the first place. "Let's take our best right fielder and make him a third baseman, since we feel Kirk Gibson should play there."

At that time, Gibson could not hit a breaking ball or handle the angles in right field at Tiger Stadium. He also would never have my arm, but he was from Michigan and I was not, and you could not help but love Gibson. Kirk could really run, and since he was a left-handed hitter, I wanted him to develop just as much as the next guy. He was also a great team leader and very demanding of himself and everyone else on the team. He had a dangerous temper, too, which made for a good guy to have on your side.

I was the bait to get the closer Sparky felt he needed to win it all in '84. We felt that we had the team to win it all, but Sparky convinced Lajoie that we still needed Willie Hernandez to bring World Series rings to Detroit. Lajoie was not going to stand up to Sparky. He did what he was told, as he mentions in his book about how Sparky would remind him that he was going to the Hall of Fame. Now we will never know if the team we had would have won the series without Hernandez.

With six days to go in spring training, while sitting at my locker, Sparky did a little wave with his finger, motioning for me to come into his office. At the same time I was walking to the office, so was John Wockenfuss. Wockenfuss, known to the Detroit fans as "Fuss," was the last guy in the world you would want to be traded with. He had a tendency be a loud mouth, would whine at times and would never have been described as my favorite teammate.

So I walked in and sat down along with Wockenfuss, Lajoie, and Sparky. Bill proceeded to explain the trade and how he appreciated our efforts. Wockenfuss went ballistic and was telling them all he had done for them and other choice statements. I never said a word. Wockenfuss stormed out, and I stood up to follow him.

Lajoie asked, "Isn't there something you wanted to say?"

"Like what?"

"Like, thank you."

That made me furious. I was their first round draft pick four years ago and had already proven I could play in the Big Leagues. Now they had traded me and you wanted me to say thank you.

"No sir, you can kiss my ass".

Honestly, why would I want to say thank you? I was coming off two really good years, and climbing my way to being an established Big Leaguer. More than that, I knew that the team I was on was about to do something great, and I wanted to be part of it. Sparky was so full of himself and was constantly over-managing and telling stories of former players from his Big Red Machine days. It made me sick. He was never in my corner, and I could not stand the guy.

I was so relieved to finally know where I was going. When I realized the Phillies were in the World Series the previous year and they had Mike Schmidt, Tug McGraw, Steve Carlton, Garry Maddox, Gary Matthews and Pete Rose, I thought I was headed to a contender. Little did I know that the Phillies were cleaning house of the "wheeze kids" and starting a youth movement. When traded, you cannot look at it as being unwanted by the team that traded you. You must look at it as being wanted by the team that gets you. I would learn this through being traded a few times over the course of my career.

The next day, I arrived in Clearwater to be a Phillie. I was greeted by a person I would come to love like a family member: Harry Kalas. Harry would end up being the only person in my baseball years that I stayed in close contact with up until his death in 2009. We would share a lot of personal things with each other, things that I was unwilling to share with anyone else in baseball. The most exciting part was meeting the face of the Phillies that I would become pretty close friends with: Mike Schmidt.

I walked into the training room and there he was, laying on a training table, getting a rub down. I asked the trainer for some tape, and as Mike heard my voice, he looked up and said, "You're the guy that was hitting all those home runs in batting practice when we played you last week."

I said yeah as he put his head back down on the table, and I walked out. I thought, "At least I made an impression on him." I mean, this was Mike Schmidt, the future hall-of-famer, and I was now one of his teammates.

He could have said welcome, but he was a very direct person with the personality of a rock. He was cocky, but not to the point of being annoying. He and I would become semi- close after the '85 season, and he asked me to share a suite with him on road-trips. I roomed with him, and we had quite the time.

Mike believed in hitting down through the ball and using all fields, although he had not always been married to that method, being a straight pull hitter early in his career. I believed in staying on the back side and trying to lift the ball and pull it. If I was late on a fastball, I could still hit it hard to right.

I learned Mike was really insecure. He disappointed me with his comment in a *Sports Illustrated* article about me by Franz Lidz entitled "This Job's A Gas". In the article that appeared in the May 1989 issue, Mike told Lidz that I was one of the top ten right fielders in the game, but "say top three because it sounds better" (Lidz, 1989). That disappointed me because that I felt that if I had not had those hundred and two RBIs in '85, Mike would not have won his third MVP award in '86, since I was the guy hitting behind him. To this day, Mike has never thanked me or acknowledged it.

I was in the lineup that first day of spring training as a Phillie, hitting fifth behind Mike. In my first at bat, I hit a double into the right center gap. I never was able to meet Pete Rose after arriving in Clearwater because he had been released and signed as a free agent with Montreal before I arrived at spring training. So since he was gone, and they had not fitted me for pants yet, they gave me Pete's. They were a perfect fit. They were long, which made them hang around my ankles. When I put them on, I remembered he wore them low around his shoes. That would be how I wore them as well. If it works for the best, why not try it?

Chapter 3

I struggled in my first year as a member of the Philadelphia Phillies. The fans and sportswriters both let me know about their dissatisfaction with the level of my play. One example of the fans letting me know they were not pleased was when a home fan keyed my car one night after I had dropped a fly ball. I was not mad about having my car keyed; more than that I was actually scared because I was in the car when it was keyed. Philly fans take their teams seriously.

Bill Conlin wrote an article about each player on the '84 roster to grade them as a player and talent. When Conlin wrote about me he said, "Glenn Wilson can't hit, can't run, and can't throw, but is a heck of a nice guy to have around the clubhouse." This infuriated me, but it also made me more determined. I thanked Bill for it later in life because it drove me to prove him wrong.

The real reason I struggled at the plate that year was because that was the year Dickie Thon had been hit in the face with a pitch by New York Mets hurler Mike Torrez. Every news station was running it over and over again, and it was embedded in my mind. The high inside pitch from Torrez had frozen Thon, and the ball slammed into his face, cracking a small bone on the orbital rim of his eye. This incident had caused Thon's eye sight to go from 20/20 before the accident to 20/150 afterward. Overtime it stabilized to 20/40, but things still seemed fuzzy. He lacked depth perception, which is important for a baseball player (Fimrite, 1990).

For the first time in my life, I was scared of the ball hitting me in the face. Our hitting coach, Darren Johnson, called me out on the bus ride to our hotel in New York by accusing me of being scared of the ball. He told me that I would have the chance to face this fear. I told him that I was not afraid, but somehow he knew and insisted that I was indeed playing scared. I finally came clean to him later that night at the hotel bar, and with tears in my eyes I admitted that he was right. He proceeded to give me some incredible wisdom by saying, "Now you can get over it."

"How?"

"The hardest part is over; you admitted it."

I would give this advice many times to other young players later in my life. I will also admit that trying to break a fear like that on your own is hard, but I am thankful that Coach Johnson called me out so I could face that fear.

I was told I would be playing left field during the '84 season instead of right field, which was my most comfortable position. I had really only played a little center and a lot of right for the Tigers in '82 and '83. The angles are different, and there are more right handed hitters in the league. In left field, the ball gets on you quicker and more balls have topspin. In my opinion, left field it is the toughest of the three outfield positions to play.

I also found facing the different pitchers in the National League for the first time tough. That year I only hit .240 and ended the season as a part-time player. The craziest incident would come late in the season, when our manager, Paul Owens, told future manager John Felske to tell me to get my glove and go play left field for the ninth inning after they had let a left-handed hitter face a left-handed pitcher. That surprised me. Since I was a bench player, they had at least been letting me hit late in games in that situation. I was mad about it, since I had never been on the bench that long. When Felske told me to get my glove and go to left, I lost it and yelled, "You go play left field mother f—." He just looked at me, shook his head, and said ok.

After the game, I was summoned into Paul Owens' office. The Pope, as he was called, asked about me not wanting to play. I told him that was not the issue; the issue was, I had been riding the pine for the last two weeks, and I was upset about it. In anger, I let him know how I felt about not playing. I told him that I was traded to Philly to play every day, and everything felt wrong. Even though I did not voice this, it was killing me inside that he Tigers, were having a great season without me. They were on their way to the playoffs and would win the World Series that year. The Pope said, "You think this is bullshit? I think the way you have played this year is bullshit!" Then he proceeded to take a swing at me. I dodged his swing, and we were wrestling on the floor for a few minutes before some coaches came in and pulled us apart.

After we had both cooled off, I told Mr. Owens, "If you'll put me back in right and leave me alone, I won't let you down."

He looked at me and said, "I respect a man that will fight for the right to play. I will honor your request, but if you let me down, I will kick your butt and then release you." I left that night with so much respect for Paul Owens that I would have run through a wall for him.

I was also on top of the world because for the first time in my young career I knew I was going to have a chance to be in the lineup every day. That's really what every player wants; to know you are going to be out on the field every day. It stinks coming to the clubhouse and having to check the lineup card to see if you are playing or not. Good managers know this struggle and are sensitive to its strain on a player's mind. Every team also needs to have those guys that are okay with being a part-time player. In my opinion, those guys should have already been everyday players, although those role players are hard to find.

Once you have been an everyday player, it is hard to be a bench player. You feel like something is missing. The right manager, though, can talk to that guy and convince him to accept a role like that. The wrong manager will say, "I am the manager and you will do what I say." That leads to the loss of respect from the player, and it can become a cancer by spreading to the other players.

Before the '85 season, John Felske was named manager, and Paul Owens was moving to the front office. It was announced that John Russell and I would be competing for the right field starting position. John Russell had come up through the Phillies system and had played for Felske in Triple A. He had hit for a high average and power in the minors as a catcher.

For the first time, I spent the winter off-season lifting weights and dedicating myself to improving my game at all costs. I knew that if I did not win that job, I would probably be out of baseball. To help speed the improvement process, I started taking steroids. Specifically, I began taking the pill form of anabolic steroids called Dianabol, which was popular around the Nautilus health clubs. It was the same drug that led to the health problems that killed former NFL players Lyle Alzado and John Matusek.

It was strange what that little pill could do; in two weeks I saw a difference in the size of my muscles. I liked it. The drug made me work harder, become more aggressive, and caused me to be quick tempered. I purchased them from a former college friend that had gone bonkers on them by transforming his body to body builder status. I purchased three bottles, a three month supply, and took them as directed. Then I never took them again. The only reason I stopped was because that winter Lyle Alzado was interviewed, and he came clean about why he was dying. His testimony saved me from using steroids ever again. Although doctors disagree on whether Alzado's steroid use led to his death, Lyle's passionate stance against them was enough.

I can understand the steroid era of baseball. While I was in Triple A in 1993, I saw my roommate sticking a needle in his butt. I asked him why he was doing that, and his response was it was the only way he was going to get to the Big Leagues because everybody in The Show was doing it. Sometimes I wonder if I was the first person to use steroids in baseball. I told a few teammates; some could tell even before I told them. I had gone from 190 pounds to 215 in three months with very little body fat. I was more confident than ever before, and I think I hit six home runs that spring. I have never heard anyone talk about their confidence during all the steroid accusations. That is the biggest thing steroids do; they make you feel invincible.

Chapter 4

I won the right field job and was off to a great start in the 1985 season. However, the team was not off to a good start, and Mike Schmidt, our star player, was hitting around .190 at the end of May. He would bounce back to hit .277, just as he had done in '84, and would collect 93 RBIs that season, but all were very surprised by his slow start. Manager John Felske was leaving me alone in right and in the five hole of the lineup. I had sixty-one RBIs at the All-star break and was originally left off the All-star team. That was very disappointing, but Pedro Guerrero would come up with an injury. During a Sunday day game in Atlanta, after getting a base hit to right in the fourth inning, I was taken out of the game.

Naturally, I was ticked until I asked John Felske what was up.

He replied, "You need to get packed for Minnesota. You made the All-Star team."

Oh my goodness, my whole body tingled, and I was completely numb. I walked up to the clubhouse where Vince Nauss had my itinerary, airline ticket, reservation, and everything else I needed to make my way to the midsummer classic. He drove me to the airport, and I could tell he was genuinely happy for me. Vince was our public relations director and traveled with the team. He would later go on to work for a baseball card company, then become a minister and eventually president of Major League Baseball Chapel.

The flight to Minnesota was delayed because of thunderstorms. I was on cloud nine and had to sit on the plane for three hours. To kill the time, I kept ordering glasses of Jack and Coke to celebrate my achievement. My pride over this career milestone grew with every drink. "Glenn Wilson, National League All-Star." It had a nice ring to it. Everyone in first class, the pilots, and the stewardesses would know me and see that I was the man. They might have even noticed I could drink a lot and not show any effects… I mean, I was the man. Big League All-Star, the big man, head honcho, big cheese, turn on your television and you could find me amongst the greatest ballplayers of my era. I was it; I had arrived and was ready to take on the world. I had money, fame, and fortune. I had achieved my goal. Did I mention I was the man? Or so I thought. When we finally took off, I was the drunk and sleeping man. My whole career, I was afraid of flying, but the drinks did the trick to help me pass out for the entire flight.

I was ridiculously superstitious as well. I never walked through an airport without stepping over every line with my right foot. That's not easy to do. If I did step on the line, I thought it would make the plane crash. I always put my right sock on first when getting dressed. I never stepped on the white line when jogging on or off a baseball field. During the "National Anthem," I would silently say the same prayer while staring at the top left star on the flag. I always wore two pair of socks and insulated long-handle underwear under my uniform.

I landed in Minnesota around midnight, and my wife Kim arrived about the same time. They took us to the hotel where we were greeted by workers that were treating us like royalty. We were taken to a room where we were given an itinerary of all the events that we would need to attend. They sized my finger for a ring. I had no idea you received a ring for being an All-Star; I thought that was really cool. Both bubbling over with excitement, Kim and I finally got into our room around two in the morning to settle into bed for the night.

The next day, a bus took the players to the stadium for a workout. The National League and American League players worked out at different times. I was glad for that because I was a little scared to see my former manager and teammates from the Tigers. Remember, they had won the World Series in 1984, and I was involved in the trade that had given them Willie Hernandez, the winner of the American League, CY Young, and MVP awards for that year. Besides being worried about that, I was anxious about being on an All-star team with players like Pete Rose, Steve Garvey, Ozzie Smith, Goose Gossage, and some guy named Nolan Ryan. This was supposed to be an exciting time, but for me, it was nerve-racking. I developed a headache that pounded my temple like a bass drum. On top of all that, the honorary captain for the National League would be Sandy Koufax. It was turning into a nightmare.

My way of dealing with stress was to make people laugh, but I could not do it there. Those were the big boys, no doubt about it. I was surrounded by the best of the best players in the world, and now I was one of them. All of this fanfare seemed almost like a dream; it was a good dream, but it caused me to feel surprisingly insecure. I remember standing in the locker room getting dressed with those guys and not saying a word.

During batting practice, the guy throwing to me was all over the place. I looked out and realized it was Mr. Koufax. This was my opportunity to make some people laugh and maybe I would relax a little, too. So I yelled out to Koufax.

"How about you throw some strikes!"

You could have heard a pin drop. He politely replied, "Bear with me; it's been awhile."

I felt like a complete jerk. I had insulted one of the greatest left-handed pitchers in the history of baseball. After batting practice, he came up to me and apologized. I assured him it was not that bad; I was just joking to try to cover my insensitivity and rudeness. He continued to say, "No son, I was plain terrible."

When you are an All-Star, they sit hundreds of baseballs before you that you have to sign. That was the one thing out of the whole experience that was not fun. I really just wanted to grab some of the balls and take them home with me. These were guys I had grown up watching, and part of me wanted their autograph. That night back at the hotel, there was a party for all the players and dignitaries of baseball. I was asked by Craig Sager of CNN to come over to their studio and talk about the upcoming game. Since I had just been with the American League two years before, they would go through the lineups while I talked about each player. I had a few beers before they asked me, so I was game.

During the interview, which was on live television, Sager asked me about Joaquin Andujar. That was the year he said, "If I isn't starting, I isn't departing." The question was how I felt about what Andujar said. Now, the last thing you do as a hitter is bash a pitcher in the newspaper or on TV, unless you do not mind getting drilled by a 95 mph fast ball. In response to his question, all I could think of was what would become my most famous quote. I said, "What one man thinks is not always the same as another." My good friend Dan Stephenson, back in Philly, has never let me forget that one.

I finished the interview and headed back to the party. I even got to meet Royals third baseman George Brett for the first time, since he could not keep his hands off my wife. The next afternoon, my wife and I went shopping and bought all kinds of All-Star memorabilia. Nobody recognized me, so it was cool shopping for items for a game you are going to play. Then it was time to get on the bus with my new friends and head over to the Metrodome for the game. I visited with Sparky and former Tiger teammate, Pitcher Jack Morris, which was really uncomfortable considering all that had taken place over the last few years.

Everything was going fine until right before we were to lineup on the first baseline for the introductions. As I was sitting on the bench daydreaming while looking out at the field, I suddenly realized that I was sitting in-between Pete Rose and Nolan Ryan. Both were holding court, as they call it, telling old stories about the Sixties and Seventies brand of baseball. I then realized where I was and the horrifying thought crossed my mind that I might have to play in the game. For the first time in a baseball uniform, I got so nervous that my stomach started churning. I grabbed my cigarettes, jumped up, and raced to the toilet…I had to GO! It was as if all of a sudden the dream I was in had ended, and I had just woken up to find out it was not a dream.

I made it back in time for the introductions and then proceeded to sit and watch the All- Stars. The most impressive thing I saw during the game was when Nolan came in to pitch. The first hitter he faced was Rickey Henderson. To my disbelief, Nolan knocked him on his ass with his first pitch. How Henderson got out of the way of that pitch is still beyond me.

Back then, even though the game was an exhibition, the National League did not look at it that way. I heard Pete give a speech before the game that would have made Knute Rockne proud. There was another party after the game, and I stayed close to my wife in case Brett showed up again. Then it was over. The whole experience had passed in a split-second, and everything seemed to have gone by way too fast. I always wished I would have made a second All-Star team so I could enjoy it without being so nervous.

The next day I had to fly to Cincinnati, and guess who I was sitting by in first class? Pete Rose. Behind him were

Dave Parker and some Italian guy that had all kinds of Pete Rose memorabilia. This was the guy that would get into some trouble later and try to drag Pete's name down with him. I believe he was also the guy that took Pete's gambling bets for him and gave him updates during Pete's gambling days. I am not positive of that, but he was shady looking.

Regarding my opinions on Pete Rose, I have never heard that he gambled on baseball during his playing career. If that is the case, then put him in the Hall of Fame. With steroids being as rampant as they were from 1993 to 2009, then Pete should go in before any of the players in that era. I also believe that there are some squeaky clean guys out there that were on the juice that are about to be eligible for induction. Anyways, I was able to listen to Pete talk baseball the whole flight, and that alone was worth making the All-Star Team.

The 1985 season would not see the Phillies make the playoffs, though I was in the hunt for 100 RBIs and a chance to lead the league in doubles. With 12 games to go in the season, I was at 91 RBIs. We were in Chicago and the wind was blowing out. In the first game of a double header, I hit my first and only Big League grand slam off Ray Fontenot. Just to ice the cake, later that game I added a solo shot off of Cubs pitcher Jay Baller (Baseball Reference).

After leaving Chicago and heading to Montreal, I only needed four RBIs. There were three games in Montreal and four left in Philly against Pittsburgh. I finished the year with 102 and could have had 105 if umpire Lee Wire did not miss a call on a fly ball to right that was trapped with the bases loaded. I sat out the final game of the season after Manager John Felske asked me if I wanted to take the day off. I still look back at that decision as stupid because I might have gained a few more RBIs if I had played that game.

I was in Philly the night I got to 100 RBIs, and it would be putting it mildly to say I got a little toasted to celebrate. The front office had sent down a bottle of champagne and a little celebration had begun. I drove from the Vet to King of Prussia, the town where I lived, totally hammered. An officer pulled me over in my subdivision, and he asked me if I had been drinking.

"Ah, no sherrrr."

"Get out of the car please." I did, and then he said something I will never forget.

"Glenn, you really should not drink and drive. By the way, congratulations on collecting your 100th RBI. You made me 100 bucks. I bet some guys at the station before the season started that you would drive in a hundred runs this year. Go on home and celebrate with your wife." So I started home.

Then he hollered, "Glenn! Aren't you forgetting something?"

"Oh, I'm sorry I forgot to give you an autograph."

"No, your car goofy! You made it this far, I think you can go two more blocks."

I did not realize I had started walking home. In those days, the cops in Philly were so cool; they knew the players and respected what we did. They knew we had huge egos and partied the way we played…hard. They were not out to make a name for themselves by destroying a guy's great day because of a bad decision.

I rarely drove drunk those days. Occasionally I would drink and drive after games, but never after more than four or five drinks. Back then, alcohol and partying was a part of baseball. Likewise, cigarettes and chewing tobacco were common vices in the clubhouse. I never had a cigarette until I got to the Big Leagues. They used to pass them out in sample packs in the clubhouse. They came five to a pack, and I remember we had so many players lighting up in the tunnel of the dugout between innings in Detroit that it was like a crowded bar. Our airplane flights with the Phillies were all chartered, and it was like a casino in the sky. Seats were pushed forward so four people could sit facing each other while the cards were dealt. The stewardesses served us steak, lobster, and sometimes themselves. There was beer in coolers and hard liquor flowing from the front to the back. It was a party every flight.

I was told that the owner of the Phillies thought I was on cocaine at one point and had me followed. I was really ticked about that because I had never tried cocaine. Len Bias' death was enough to remind me of the deadly consequences of cocaine, and it was not something I was willing to risk. I was scared of coke, but I did try marijuana once. It made me too paranoid, and I could never escape the voice from my childhood of my oldest brother Johnie telling me that if he ever caught me doing drugs, he would kill me.

I did, however, get invited to a party that year on a road trip to Chicago. I was told it was to see one of the big boxing matches of Sugar Ray Leonard. I was there with some pretty big names in the game, even some from other teams in Chicago. They brought out a huge bag of what I knew was weed, and then a big jar of some white powder. I calmly told a person that was there, who was a future Hall of Famer, that I didn't do that stuff and wanted to leave. He agreed to let me go but reminded me that what you see here stays here. It was just like the unwritten clubhouse rule: nothing was to be shared. I said no problem and left the party. I headed over to Rush Street where I proceeded to get wound up on Jack and Coke. I am not saying I was better than those guys that did the white stuff; I wasn't. I was still diving into a bottle of Jack for the purpose of being inebriated. It was the vice that I was comfortable with, but I was just as guilty.

Chapter 5

After the '85 season, the Phillies rewarded me with a three-year contract worth two million dollars. Kim and I were able to have a house in Texas and a townhouse in Philly. We had one son and another son on the way. I wanted our kids to go to school in Texas. I had also promised Kim's mom I would never take her daughter too far away from home.

The winter before the '86 season, out of nowhere, John Felske announced to the media that I would be hitting fourth and Schmidt would be moved back to fifth. I was a little shocked, but boy was my chest bowed out. Just thinking about all the fastballs I would be seeing by hitting in front of

Mike still makes my hair stand up. Of course, after only one day at spring training, Mike went to the manager and the lineup was quickly changed back to me at five and Mike four. I still wonder to this day what Mike said to get this changed.

The '86 season was not as good for me as '85, because I started off slow, hitting about .180 at the end of May. John Felske said something no manager had or would say to me my entire career. I had driven in 100 runs the year before for him, and I was going to be in the lineup everyday unless I asked for a day off. The moment he said that, I went on a tear. I would end up driving in eighty-six runs and hitting around .270. I led the league in outfield assists again, but this year with twenty.

I was surprised teams were still trying to run on me. I remember being in right field at Veterans Stadium and trying to think of ways to get some attention. I started trying to throw runners out at first base on a clean base hit. I would tell Von Hayes, "Be ready now. If there is a hard hit ball on the ground to right, I may come up firing, so be ready." I tried it a couple of times on a grass field and was not even close. On turf though, I knew I could get a slow runner.

The first guy I gunned was Keith Moreland. He was embarrassed, but the fans loved it. Then I got Nick Esasky after he rounded the bag. I figured out that when a player was making his turn on a base hit to right, he would make that smooth cool turn and then retreat easily back to the bag. I had so much confidence in my arm strength and accuracy that if I threw it at his head, he would fall forward to get out of the way. Then my first baseman would catch the head-height throw and apply the tag. The one with Esasky was awesome because it was the last out of a game that we won in the ninth.

I got Esasky because he was slow, like Moreland, but I even did the unthinkable by picking off the speedy Otis Nixon. One night, he was on second when a sharp one-hop line drive was hit to me in right. I knew the third base coach for Montreal, Russ Nixon, would not send Otis with my arm.

I slightly stumbled as I fielded the ball and threw a strike to Schmidt at third as Nixon was rounding the bag. When Nixon looked up and saw Schmidt with the ball he was in shock. He at least made the infielders make three throws in the rundown, but he was dead meat. The fans went nuts, all to my joy. I feel that to this day, because I was throwing guys out in creative ways, it kept me in the lineup when I was not hitting. Once I was playing against Houston and Nolan Ryan got a hit to right, and I could have nailed him easily, but since I did not want one of his fastballs in my ear, I calmly made an easy throw into second. I remember my teammates laughing their butts off.

Since I was now an all-star, I was also able to get away with saying a little more to umpires than I could in the past. One night we were in St. Louis, with "Balking" Bob Davidson behind home plate and Todd Worrell in to close out the game for the Cardinals. After the first pitch was six inches or so outside for a called strike, I let him know that ball was not a strike. Bob took off his mask and yelled in my ear, telling me that I had been complaining for two weeks.

We had been stuck with the same crew for two weeks, and I probably had been complaining a little too much. I did not look back at Bob or say anything while he had his say. When he was finished and went back behind the plate, I calmly turned towards him, flipped my bat in the air, caught it with the handle facing him, and politely said, "Oh, is that so? Then you try to hit that shit."

He proceeded to give me the wave that signified, "You're out of here!" When he did, he hit himself in the back of the head and his hat came off. That's when I started screaming, "You see how bad your ejection was? That's how bad your plate calling has been!"

Since I was undoubtedly ejected, Greg Gross replaced me at the plate and secured a base hit to start a rally. I knew I was not going to touch Worrell that night.

The '87 season was a disaster; I only had fifty-four RBIs, though my average was still around .270. The big difference was we had acquired Lance Parrish and Mike Easler, and Manager John Felske had them hitting in front of me in the order. I was now hitting 7th in front of Steve Jeltz. I liked Steve, but he was a glove shortstop and not much with the stick. Since I was an aggressive hitter, this meant I needed to develop more patience at the plate, which was something I did not do well.

My home run totals were close to the same, but the drop in RBIs meant I was once again trade bait. The new manager, Lee Elia, liked me as a player, but I think he expected too much production out of me in that spot when he dropped me in the order. That winter, the Phillies hired a new GM named Lee Thomas; I was the first to go. I had become very popular in Philadelphia as a mainstay in right field for three years. Many of the fans in Philly even knew me as "Glennbo" because of the promotional TV commercials the team made of me dressed as John Rambo from the movie Rambo. I loved Philadelphia and wanted to finish my career there. This move hurt my career more than any of all the trades I experienced.

I really felt Phillies Owner Bill Giles cared about my family and me, but baseball is a business run by people that never played the game. It is still this way in most cities, where the mindset is, "Let's spend millions of dollars but let a person that never played the game in the Big Leagues be the general manager and field manager." The philosophy behind this is that their status as great businessmen somehow qualifies them to run a baseball team because it is composed of twenty-five guys who are making big money. I never understood why you would hire a person that could not play the game. Their lack of experience means they have no idea what a player can be feeling or going through during a one hundred and sixty-two game schedule. To me that is like saying, "Well, I can coach the Dallas Cowboys because I watched a lot of football on TV." There is no replacement for experience.

I knew one of the things I would miss the most about being a Phillie was being part of all the practical jokes that happened in the clubhouse. I loved making people laugh, though I made some guys mad at times. For example, one time Chris James brought some watermelons to the clubhouse when we were playing the Astros in Houston. He had stayed at his home, as did I, and we drove our own cars to the visiting stadium, arriving at the same time. His dad had a watermelon patch and he was bringing some in for the team. I helped him carry them into the locker-room. I had the bright idea of putting one in each of the black guy's lockers. They did not find that one funny as a few of them chased me around the Astrodome all batting practice, but it was all done in fun.

Sometimes the jokes were on me, like when Steve Carlton, John Wockenfuss, and some others were shooting a compound bow in the clubhouse in Philly. When I saw this, I thought, "Let's go outside and shoot an arrow into the center field fence."

I knew very little about compound bows, so Carlton said I had to aim higher to hit the centerfield wall. He told me the arrow would tear the turf if I aimed straight at it, so I aimed higher. He kept telling me higher until I was aiming up out of the stadium. That's right where that arrow went… "Outta here!" as Harry Kalas would have called it.

I swear I could not sleep for two nights, thinking I might have shot a guy that was driving down the school expressway through the heart with an arrow. I would miss being a part of a group of guys who had so much fun and an organization that treated you like family while you were there. Most of all, I would miss being around the late Harry Kalas, he was a great friend and we had too much fun.

This time I was traded to Seattle for a .300 hitter named Phil Bradley. Phil had also been a participant in the 1985 All-Star game representing Seattle as a member of the American League team. When Bill Giles called me on the evening of December 9th to inform me of the trade, I was devastated. Back then, Seattle was like a Triple A team. I did not even know where it was on the map. In order to drown my sorrows that night, I drank a six-pack of Corona beer, forgetting that I had been taking allergy medicine. The medicine specifically warned against consuming alcohol on the box, but in my pain the warnings on the medicine box were the last thing to cross my mind.

The next morning, I was on the phone talking to a sports writer from Seattle when I felt my heart skip a beat. My heart continued to skip beats as we talked… first one, then another. All of a sudden it seemed to completely stop beating for a second. I calmly asked the reporter if I could call him back. I sat near the fireplace and told my wife Kim something was not right. I started to get scared, and then I started to panic. I told Kim I needed to get to a hospital.

She said, "Well, I can't go looking like this, I haven't showered."

"While I go die of a heart attack, you get dressed."

I jumped in my Porsche and told my friend HB that was over at the house to get in and ride with me. I drove 100 mph on a road designed for 35 mph trying to get to the hospital as soon as possible.

I will never forget seeing my kids playing in the side yard as I was leaving and wondering if this would be the last time I would see them. I made it to the local clinic and after they took my blood pressure, they immediately loaded me into an ambulance. While on the stretcher, I asked them to wait a second before they put me in; I wanted to see the sun one more time. I have no idea why I asked that other than I thought I was going to die. The whole ride I kept asking the doctor if I was about to die, and they were not answering me. I could tell by the looks on their faces and the way they were acting that this was serious.

I was in what is called atrial fibrillation, which is an abnormal heart rhythm. While atrial fibrillation can at times be asymptomatic, I would stay in this condition for twelve hours. To tolerate the chest pain, the doctors pumped me full of pain medication so that I could only feel my heart skipping beats.

When they got me back to a normal rhythm, they said they wanted to keep me in the hospital overnight. By now my oldest brother Johnie was there, and Kim was not far behind. Johnie was worried about the media finding out because he felt if they did, I might not be able to play baseball anymore. He stayed at my door all night. Looking back, both the Mariners and Phillies would have had to make a decision whether or not to let the trade go through if my physical condition had been revealed. Not even my agents were informed to ensure that my career would not be affected.

The next day, my doctor visited me and informed me I was fine. He believed it was an isolated incident, and I had no reason to worry. I said, "Doc that can't be; there is a real problem, and you must be missing it." He insisted I was fine and I was being released. I could not accept his decision. A couple of days went by, and I began to have palpitations again. Every time I did, I was overcome with fear.

I remember one time I was driving into town and the palpitations would not go away. I pulled my car over on the side of the road and just sat there and cried. With my wife's encouragement, I decided to see a heart specialist. The heart specialist was a doctor that my mother-in-law had known a long time, Dick Cashion. He had worked under Dr. Michael DeBakey, the doctor who had performed the first heart transplant. Dr. Cashion performed a myriad of tests and came to the same conclusion: I was fine. I kept insisting that something was really wrong and lamented that I was sure that he was overlooking my condition. He decided to put me on a drug called Corgard. He said it would help with the palpitations and keep my blood pressure down when I was having anxiety. What he forgot to tell me was about the side effects, which included sluggishness and slower reflexes; neither were things that were assets to a Major League hitter.

I headed off to Seattle on the last year of my contract, where the Mariners were counting on me to be their cleanup hitter. Since my father had died at the age of forty-one, I assumed an early death was a certainty for me. I never told the Mariners anything. To begin the season, I started zero for my first twenty-one at bats. This was not the impression I wanted to make on my new team, especially being on the last year of my contract.

We were a bad team, although we really had a good nucleus with Alvin Davis, Harold Reynolds, Mark Langston, and Jim Presley. We also had a veteran manager, Dick Williams, a man that seemed to almost hate life. The Mariners also had a Triple A player at spring training named Ken Griffey, Jr. When I saw the kid, I was not impressed. I thought he would never make it in the Big Leagues, and he certainly would never be seen as the same caliber player as his father… so much for me being a scout.

One of the funniest things I ever pulled in the Bigs was at the Kingdome. I was playing right field with the bases loaded in a game against the Texas Rangers. A ball was sliced down the first base line, hooking along the ground. The bullpen was down in this area about thirty feet from the foul line. The bullpen benches were there as well; a place for the relief pitchers to sit and wait to be called into action. The ruling was even if a ball lodged behind the bench, it was still in play. While I was running toward the bullpen, I saw the ball lodge behind the bench right behind the bullpen ball bag. Rather than waste any time trying to dig the ball out from behind the bench, I reached in the ball bag, grabbed a ball, fired to third, and nailed the runner who was running from first for an out.

At that time, Bobby Valentine was the Rangers' manager. Told by three left-handed pitchers of what I had done, Valentine went to discuss this with the umpires. They looked at the ball, and since they could not tell any difference in the ball, my team was awarded the out. After the game, a couple of reporters asked me if I had actually reached in the ball bag and grabbed a ball. My reply was, "Look. I raced into the bullpen, grabbed the first ball I saw that had Bobby Brown's name on it, and came up throwing." Bobby Brown was the

American League president at the time, and his signature was on every American League ball. I still think it was awesome to be able to think that fast and get away with it.

The only other highlight I had while being a Mariner was I finally hit a home run over the Green Monster at Fenway Park in Boston. That was special because of all those games I had seen on TV when I was a kid.

The rest of my time in Seattle was pretty horrific. I would have scary mood swings because even though I was doing what I loved, I hated it in Seattle and wanted out. I also felt that the Mariners should have picked up the option year on my contract when they traded for me, just as I heard the Phillies had done for Phil Bradley after our trade. Since they did not decide to pick up my option and I was not too fond of the American League, I went to the newspapers and made my point clear... I WANTED OUT! It worked; I had pissed off the front office enough that I was traded to Pittsburgh a couple of weeks later.

The tough part about the timing of this trade was I was traded the day before the father-son game. This is where the kids of the players get to come on the field before the game and play against their dads. When I got home and told my family of the trade, my oldest son, Glenn Jr., was terribly upset, not about the trade, but about having to miss the father-son game. So I called the Pirates, and thank God, they had not had their father-son game. I guess you could say both my son and I got traded, and we were both happy.

I arrived in Pittsburgh the day after the trade and was in the lineup with Van Slyke, Bonilla, and Bonds. I felt I had never left the National League. I was thrilled, especially since the traded reunited me with my old Triple A Manager, Jim Leyland.

Before I was traded, Leyland had done what is called tampering. Since he knew me personally, he had called me a couple of times to make sure I was healthy. This time I was traded for Darnell Coles, an outfielder that was a pretty solid player. While in Pittsburgh, I did not rent a place since it was already August; I stayed downtown at the Vista hotel. It was a nice place and was within walking distance of the ballpark.

On the positive side, I finished the 1988 season by hitting .270 and playing a solid right field, but ended the year in my time in Seattle and Pittsburgh combined with only five home runs, the lowest total of my career.

One night, during a home game against Montreal, I was almost plunked by a pitch that was high and tight. In trying to move out of the way of the pitch, I bent my right knee all the way back with my cleat in the ground; all of my weight shifted to that leg, and I landed awkwardly. I felt no pain after the game, so I walked home to the hotel. When I woke up and began to get out of the bed the next morning, I could not move my leg due to the pain. I phoned the trainer and an ambulance came and took me to the hospital.

Ray Miller, the Pirates pitching coach, had a great laugh at my expense. In an act of clubhouse humor, he was telling everyone that I must have stopped at one of the local bars on the way home and fell through the bridge over the Alleghany River. I was in and out of the hospital in two days and back playing in ten days thanks to the best trainer in baseball, Kent Biggerstaff. He was relentless at getting a player to push himself through an injury.

That off season, with collusion still going on, the Pirates decided not to pick up my option at $850,000. They instead made me an offer of $650,000 for two years. This amount was a pay cut of $100,000 from my previous year's salary. My agents said there were no other teams showing interest and advised me to take it, so in my mind I was prepared to be a Bucco for the next two years.

Of course every time I began to feel comfortable with where I was in my career then things would get interesting again and that is exactly what happened in Pittsburgh. In May, our catcher Mike LaValliere was injured on a play at the plate. His knee would require surgery and he would be lost for most, if not all, of the season. That meant back-up catcher Junior Ortiz was playing every day. He was solid but not a front line guy. The Pirates went in search of a starting catcher. Guess who the bait would be? That's right… here we go again.

Early in the 1989 season, I had been hot with the bat. I was leading the team in RBIs and was close to the top in home runs, which meant I also had a higher than usual batting average at the time. The fact I was playing so well had all the makings for me being solid trade bait. During this season, I got hot with a ten-game hitting streak while eating at McDonalds every day. With my superstitious nature and recent success in the midst of a McDonald eating marathon, my newest superstition was born. My McDonalds' streak made national news, and when one of the local McDonalds heard about it, they began sending Big Macs to the clubhouse before games for the entire team. While in that type of streak, you get real quiet and try to stay in the zone.

When my average had risen above .300, that was the highest it had been since my rookie year. I was really quiet then, sitting in the clubhouse between innings, smoking a cigarette with Ray Miller beside me. One of the grounds crew guys walked by us and said, "Hey, Willie! How's it going?" Normally, I would have just said "Hi" during a streak like that, but I could not resist with Ray sitting there.

"Pretty good buddy."

Ray looked at me, and we both knew that I had just broken my streak. It is just one of those baseball superstitions, like when a pitcher has a no-hitter; you just don't talk about it.

Rumors were circulating that Houston might be my next destination. Our next series was in San Diego for four games on a weekend, and after the Saturday night game Leyland summoned me to his office. He explained that I had been traded to Houston, and since he and I were friends from my Triple A days, he asked me if I was ok with it. I said sure; it was my hometown, and I think most players secretly or openly dream of playing in their hometown. I told Jim I would miss him all the way until those wheels touched down in Houston. He laughed and so did I as I walked out of his office.

Even though I was excited about playing in my hometown, I found myself at that familiar spot of being comfortable and established in Pittsburgh and subsequently being traded. I was being traded for Alan Ashby, the Astros starting catcher. Ashby had the same agent as me, so I got a call that night from Alan Hendricks. He told me the trade was not going to happen. Ashby was a five and ten guy, meaning five years with the same team and ten years in the Big Leagues, so he had the power to turn the trade down. I understood his reasons for not wanting to leave Houston; his family was established there, and his kids were enrolled in school. I really wanted the trade to happen because I wanted to play at home and was ticked at the Pirates for not wanting me anymore.

No one knew what was about to happen. Ashby declined the trade even after the Pirates offered him another year on his contract. Alan's veto of the trade did not sit well with the Astros. Needless to say, I was also disappointed. I had gone as far as to have our agent, tell Ashby that I would give him $50,000 of my own money to accept it. He still refused, and on that next Sunday, when the Astros were loaded on the bus for a road trip, they called Ashby off the bus to tell him he had been released. That was low by any standards. I remember thinking that the game is cruel. People in power could care less about you the person; they only cared about what you could do for them on the field, and you better not tick them off.

Speaking of pissed off, the next day, which was that dreadful Sunday for Ashby, I had to show up at Jack Murphy stadium and get dressed as a Pirate. This is the part that got all over me. While sitting on the dugout bench, waiting to take batting practice, my so-called friend Jim Leyland came and sat by me and had the nerve to ask me what happened. I said in disgust, "Well, last night you traded me, and today you have me in your lineup."

He replied, "And I'm counting on you, too."

I was so ticked, I wanted to knock him out. I felt like a piece of meat; an unwanted, unappreciated piece of meat that was hung out to dry.

When I was in Philadelphia back in 1985, we had a coach named Dave Bristol who would go out of his way to piss me off about every two or three days. What I found out later was Bristol knew that if I was pissed off, I would probably have a good game. It is people like that in the game that are often over-looked. For some reason, he knew this about me. I can remember many times when I played a game so mad I could fight and wound up having a great game. The more I thought about the fact I had lost the chance to play for my hometown team, the more my anger grew. My anger was so intense that it led me to commit the unpardonable sin of baseball; I went over the manager's head to the GM.

At that time in Pittsburgh, the GM was a very nice man named Larry Doughty. When I told him that Leyland told me I was traded before the deal was done, he acted as if he was ticked at Leyland. I continued to play right field pretty much every day and was producing fairly well. Then August came around and while in Atlanta, Larry called me up to his hotel room and to ask me what would make me a very happy man.

"Being traded to Houston."

"That is precisely what I have done, and in return we are getting Billy Hatcher."

It seemed to me that the Astros really wanted me, and I was excited to go home and play in the Astrodome where I used to watch games in high school. It was surreal the first time I walked onto the field as a member of the Astros. I remember telling my friends in high school that someday they would see my name on that scoreboard.

When meeting some of my new teammates I jokingly said, "Ok boys, you can relax now. I'm here, so the pennant is a lock." That joke did not go over as well as I imagined it would since Billy Hatcher was wildly popular amongst his teammates. I was immediately their new starting right fielder, and they moved Kevin Bass to left.

My first full season in Houston in 1990 would be one of misery. Two years prior, I had bought a gas station in Montgomery, Texas, where my wife and I made our home in the off- season. I hired a friend I had met on a hunting trip to Wyoming named Hal Bent to run it and I would work at my station in the off-season. That winter before the 1990 season, my wife had a miscarriage, which would have been our third son (later we would find out it was actually twin boys we lost). My wife was severely depressed after the miscarriage, and seeking to help her cope, I called my agents, the Hendricks brothers, to ask if I could afford a new and bigger house. I thought a new house would get her busy, raise her spirits, and keep her mind off the miscarriage. It would also get us closer to Houston, since we lived over an hour from the Astrodome.

Alan Hendricks said that the Astros were going to give me a three-year contract extension and that we would be fine. They even said the Astros extension would be in the range of $1.3 million a year for three years. We found a house in The Woodlands and made the purchase. The Hendricks brothers handled all my finances, meaning my checks went to their offices and they paid my bills. If I needed anything, I would ask for their blessing. When purchasing something like a house, I felt like a rap star at the closing, having two attorneys, a CPA, and one or two secretaries.

They also handled investing for me, although none of their investing turned out anywhere close to what they had promised me. This is how their investing conversations went: "Glenn, this is Alan or Randy. I am sending you some investment opportunities. When they arrive, call me so I can tell you what pages you need to sign on. It will be making you more money than you're making playing baseball."

Then, after my career as a player was almost over, the IRS disallowed those seven to one tax write-off investments. I am not saying that my agents stole money or cheated me out of money, but I am saying that I think they were learning how to be agents at the time.

We moved into the new house about a month before the 1990 spring training was to start. I still had not received the contract extension I was told I would be getting. Then, out of nowhere, the owners locked us out of spring training. When the lockout was over, we were only allowed two-week spring training. Personally, that was and is plenty of time to get ready for a Major League season. As a result of the lockout and the cost of rising salaries, the owner of the Astros, John McMullen, placed the team up for sale.

I was informed by my agents that the contract extension would not be coming. What was worse: if the team did not get off to a good start, the management would be dumping salaries.

The team broke out of the gates badly by only winning twenty of our first fifty games. I was now expendable as they had been playing me less to make room for a young player named Eric Anthony, a left-handed power hitter, who just so happened to be a right fielder. On May 17, 1990, Anthony did a feat only a few had ever done in the Astrodome. He hit a ball into the rainbow seats of the Astrodome off of Chicago Cubs Pitcher pitcher Mike Bielecki (Baseball Reference). As the ball was travelling into the bleachers, I remember thinking I would be seeing more time on the pine over the next few weeks. Anthony had been receiving a good chunk of the time in right field during the 1990 season, so that meant more time for me in left field or riding the bench.

Since things were going the way they were, I decided I had enough and took it upon myself to ask for a meeting with the General Manager, Bill Wood, and field manager, Art Howe on June 18, 1990. In the meeting, I pleaded my case about playing time and being a free agent at the end of the year, but they made it clear to me that I would be doing whatever was asked of me. I proceeded to call the GM a liar and Art an idiot. I even challenged the GM to a fight in the parking lot. I felt betrayed because of that three-year contract extension that Alan Hendricks said they offered before the season. Now I was just sitting the bench and would be a free agent at the end of the year.

Then Anthony tweaked a hamstring somehow before that night's game, so I was in the lineup. As fate would have it, that was just about the best all around series of games I had in my career. I had three hits in the game on the 18th, one of which was a home run off Dodgers' pitcher Tim Belcher (Baseball Reference). Then after the game, when I was being interviewed by Bill Worrell, I wanted to blast the Astros. I knew that would be the kiss of death. So I just kept answering his questions with, "It was just nice to be back in the lineup and contribute." In that series I also made three diving catches, including one that saved the game in the ninth inning. I also threw out Kirk Gibson at home plate for the 100th outfield assist for my career.

The 1990 season was Art Howe's second year to manage in major league baseball. I was frustrated with the whole situation. We were playing in New York one night when in the fourth inning while I was leading the team in RBIs batting cleanup, Art made a double switch. I thought, "What is he doing?" I mean, he made out the lineup, and I was his cleanup hitter. After the double switch, it was obvious that he did not care or did not have a clue that he had just embarrassed me. I held a grudge against Art for that one move for a long time.

Later that year, he made a mistake with the lineup cards. The lineup card he gave the umpire did not match the lineup card posted in the dugout. This cost the team a base runner, and I believe that was ultimately the dagger that cost Art his job in Houston. In spite of my displeasure with some of his moves, Art was and still is one of the nicest people you will ever meet in all of baseball.

One of the funniest moments that happened during my stint with Houston happened after the '89 season when I was working out at the Astrodome. The Astros hired a new hitting coach that my teammates and I had never heard of named Rudy Jaramillo. While I was hitting in the cage underneath the bleachers, Rudy walked up and started to watch me hit. Rudy was about as clueless about me as I was about him. As I was hitting, he asked me, a nine-year Major League veteran, where I played last year. In response to his bad question, I sarcastically answered, "Double A, I hit .239. What do you think of my swing? Do you think I have a chance to make it to the Big Leagues?" I proceeded to act really goofy, changing my stance constantly and trying to look as bad as possible. When I got through, he just said to keep working and he would help me over the next couple of weeks.

After that hitting session, I caught Art in his office and told him that Rudy did not know who I was. I asked Art not to tell him because I wanted to have some fun with this situation. After about four days of this charade, it became so comical that I finally let the cat out of the bag. I laughed my butt off, but I could tell Rudy was embarrassed. Welcome to the Big Leagues rookie.

At the end of the 1990 season, I leaped for a ball in Wrigley Field, and landed on the pitching rubber of the bullpen mound down the right field line. I developed severe pain in my right knee when I would try to run at full speed. September 1st was approaching, and the Astros were dumping players left and right to cut payroll. I had gotten wind of a rumor that the Mets were interested in trading for me to help them on the stretch run. In the past, I was the best at hiding injuries and would never be caught dead in the trainer's room. To keep the injury a secret, I would go to an outside doctor, get a shot, and keep playing with that area numbed. This time it did not work as the Astros realized I was hurt and they were not happy about it. So they suggested, "Let us shoot you up." So I allowed them to give me pain shots three times over the process of two days.

Even with the pain shots, I still could not run. Since they could not trade me now, they scheduled an arthroscopic procedure the day after the trade deadline. To me these procedures were no big deal as over my career this was my fourth time. I still wonder to this day what went wrong.

When I awoke from the anesthesia from the surgery, I had a cast on my leg.

Were the Astros so ticked at me they purposely opened me up so I would not be able to get a job the next year? Or had I been playing with a terrible knee, numbing it up causing it to get worse? The doctor said that while in surgery, they decided to do what was called a lateral release, because I had displaced my kneecap.

It would not surprise me if the doctor was ordered to cut the leg off and make something up regarding my condition. It may sound paranoid, but that's how some of these front office guys in Major League organizations operate; either play by my rules or pay the consequences. Think about it, if a GM is making hundreds of thousands of dollars and a player makes him look bad to the owner; what do you do? Ruin the guy.

I spent six months rehabbing that knee. I was now thirty-one years old, and I had no contract, not to mention the fact that I was coming off a surgery. Worried that I would be overlooked, I wore my agent's phone out that winter. This was also the year that the damaged collusion players were awarded free agency. My agents had what seemed like thirteen pitchers, so you can guess where I was on their list of priorities.

It was now mid-February, and I still didn't have a job. I personally started calling managers, and I spoke with Bobby Cox whose exact words were, "Glenn, I didn't even know you were a free agent."

I had a contract with Atlanta in two days; there was no guarantee, but I was offered $150,000 to come to spring training. If I made the Big Club, I would make the same thing I had made the year before while with the Astros, $750,000.

As spring training went on with the Braves, it was getting to be crunch time. I had tried to fire my agents, but they threatened me with an incident surrounding some girl who was claiming I had gotten her pregnant years ago. I remembered the incident they were talking about, but I also knew what it took to get a girl pregnant. I am not saying

I did not make mistakes on road trips, but I know what I did and did not do. Then they also said, "Nobody leaves the Hendricks." I felt like I was in a *Sopranos* episode.

The Braves roster was down to two players for one spot; their greatest need was a right-handed pinch hitter. It had come down to Andres Thomas and me for this last spot on the Braves roster. I watched a coach call Thomas into the office, and then watched him pack his belongings. I was elated because seeing him pack meant that I was going to get to stay in Atlanta. So when Bobby Cox and John Schuerholz called me into the office, I thought it was to sign my contract.

John said, "Glenn, we have a problem." Since I was the only player left and thought I was about to sign my contract, I was in a good mood.

"How can I help?"

"We traded for Otis Nixon in the eleventh hour last night."

"That's great; he can really help us."

Bobby Cox spoke up and said, "Glenn, you don't understand."

"Yes, I do. That guy can fly. He's really going to help us out."

"This makes you the odd guy out," Bobby informed me.

Wow. For the first time in nine consecutive years, I was not going to be on a Big League team. I was in shock. Then John shared his plan, "We would like for you to go to Triple A Richmond."

"Wow…I don't know. I've been in the Big Leagues for the last nine years."

"Go home and think about it, and give us a call in a couple of days. We'll pay you that $150,000 while you're in Triple A." He was trying to cut a deal at the lowest moment of my life.

I spoke up and said, "Mr. Schuerholz, you already owe me $150,000 just for coming to spring training."

"Oh yeah, that's right," he responded, acting like he had forgotten.

"Now, if you want me to go to Triple A, we can discuss a contract for that scenario."

"Well, I don't even know what Triple A players make for a season these days."

"Nice try, but I do. A guy with my experience is around $10,000 a month. So when I get home and talk to my wife, I will call you and we can discuss it."

"That would be fine."

Now for the first time in nine years, I was without a team in The Show. I packed my belongings and headed out the dugout exit. I had to walk across the field to the parking lot where my car was parked. The next moment I will never forget; as I was walking across the field, home plate caught my eye, and I walked towards it. I stepped right on it and remember thinking that was it; I was done as a baseball player. I thought, "This very well could be my last trip to home plate on a major league field." Was my journey done?

When I got to my car, I cried like I was at a family member's funeral. I went to the hotel and proceeded to drink the rest of the day away. This life, this dream, this journey; I knew it was over.

The next day, I caught a flight home and talked with my wife. Since I had so much stupid pride, I thought there was no way I could go to Triple A. After two days at home and talking it over, I had decided to hang it up. But when the phone rang and John Schuerholz was on the other end, I told him the exact opposite, assuring him I would report to Richmond. He offered me the $10,000 a month and said the $150,000 was in the mail. That was the best negotiating I would ever do over the course of my career; sometimes when you really don't try, it just seems to work out. The only thing I told him was that I wanted to be a free agent while in Triple A, and I would only be there six weeks. If I did not have a job in the Bigs within that timeframe, then I would retire. So I met the team in Richmond and started playing.

The six weeks went by and no Big League job materialized. After a Sunday afternoon day game, I met with my old friend and farm director Bill Lajoie, along with Joe Niekro, who was the manager in Richmond. I told them I would not be making the trip to Tidewater the next day. They both said I would be there, but I assured them that I would not be in attendance. Back at my apartment that evening, I called HB, the manager of my gas station, and told him to send someone to drive my car; I was taking a flight home. So in that split second I made one of my worst choices of my career... I quit. Two to three weeks later David Justice went down with an injury, and I could have been the guy they called up.

Chapter 6

I arrived home and started learning to play golf. For the rest of that year, I played golf almost every day. My wife had started her own decorating business, and she loved it. To my excitement, I was invited to spring training with the Texas Rangers in early 1992.

While at Rangers' spring training, where they had me working with the Triple A team, I remember walking over to the stadium where the Big Leaguers played their games. I watched guys like Pudge Rodriguez and Juan Gonzalez, and

I thought to myself that those guys were huge and I could not compete with them. Before spring training ended, Marty Scott, the farm director, said there was a team in Mexico that wanted to sign me, and the Rangers were not going to need me; not even with the Triple A club. I said thanks, but no thanks, even though Scott said they would pay me $10,000 a month; I did not want to play in Mexico.

So once again, I was back at home spending all my free moments on the golf course. By now, I had lowered my handicap down to a ten and was playing in some pretty hefty money games with some guys I met who were about ten years older than me. It was competition that fed the fire I missed of being out on the baseball field.

I had not played in the Big Leagues for two years, but in the spring of 1993, I got a call from Ted Simmons, the new GM of the Pirates. Over the phone, Ted, a former major leaguer himself, told me that he would like me to come to spring training. He said that he did not understand how I could pass up this opportunity, because the Pirates were dumping salaries. If I could still hit, they would bring me up as a right-handed pinch hitter off the bench. The thought of getting another chance to play in the Bigs was intriguing, so I said I would get in shape and report to the team.

I had never worked that hard in my life to get into shape. I was thirty-four now, and I needed to be in the best shape I could be in to deal with the grind of the major league season. No, I did not call my old friend about the steroids, but I probably would have if the drugs did not scare me. I went to camp and had Doc Edwards as my Triple A manager, a man I grew to respect very quickly. When it came down to the final cuts, Doc decided he wanted me on his club. So I shuffled off to Buffalo with the rest of the Triple A hopefuls.

At this point in my career, I only needed seventy days in the Big Leagues to have the full ten years to be eligible for the maximum pension. I was off to a good start with the bat, and with Doc Edwards playing as designated hitter more than right field; I was able to save my legs. The legs are the first part of the body that starts to go for position players in their early thirties.

I remember a funny thing that happened one night during a home game. I was in right field, and a line drive was hit to my right. I was in a dead run when I realized that if I did not slide for this ball, it would get to the wall. The grass was wet, because it rains a lot in early April in Buffalo. I progressed into my slide, scooped the ball, planted my right foot, and came up firing to second. I nailed the rookie, and since it was the third out, I started jogging off the field. After walking in the dugout and sitting at the end of the bench, I overheard Doc telling some of the players that back in my prime I would not have had to slide for that ball. He told them I would have nailed the guy by ten feet. It was funny because in my mind, it was a better play and throw than any I had made in my prime.

I never said anything to anyone, but to this day, I have never thought about the fact of whether or not I was in my prime or not; I just tried to make the plays. Either I was really good in my twenties, or I was thinking too highly of myself in my early thirties, but I never saw much difference in my game.

There was a team meeting that Doc held one day before a game. I was so taken off guard by what he said that I had to think about it for a long time. Most managers would start their meetings with some kind of talk about what we need to do as a team, or why the team is not playing well. This meeting was no different. As Doc started, I was drifting off, thinking about something else. All of a sudden, Doc grew loud and said, "And this guy right here," pointing at me, "is going to be a great manager some day." What in the world? Where did that come from? I had never even thought of managing. Wouldn't you know, after my career was over I did manage four years of Independent Minor League ball, and three of those teams made it to the championship series.

In late April, the Pirates' big club came to town to play an exhibition game. We had a Home Run Derby before the game. There was Leyland over in the other dugout; I had not spoken to him since the trade to Houston back in 1989. When he came over to our dugout, he never even acknowledged me. Needless to say, I did not try to speak to him. The Home Run Derby was won by Lonnie Smith who beat me out by one home run.

During the game, I had a couple of hits and one RBI. Afterwards, Ted Simmons, the general manager of the Pirates, came over to our clubhouse to visit with me.

He asked me, "What did you do to piss Leyland off?"

"I have no idea." I really did, but I did not want to tell the guy who could bring me up to the big leagues.

"Well, I am trying to bring you up because you can still hit, but Leyland hates your guts."

"Wow, I wonder why?"

"I will get this worked out; just don't pull anything."

One week went by…then two.

My wife and two oldest sons flew into Nashville, where we were about to start a weekend series. While hanging out by the pool with my wife and kids that Saturday, Doc walked over and met them. Then he informed me, "Oh, by the way, they need you with the Big Club."

I grinned and was as excited as when I was called up my rookie year twelve years prior. I think Doc enjoyed telling us as much as we enjoyed hearing it. Then he said, "You leave in the morning, and I'm not going to play you tonight because I don't want you to pull a muscle or something."

I calmly sat on the bench and just watched the Bisons and Sounds play a game until the ninth inning. In the ninth, our outfielder, Will Pennyfeather, got thrown out of the game. Doc had no other choice but to tell me to go to right. Going for a fly in shallow right, I strained a hamstring. If I told the trainer, I would not go to The Show, so I just kept it quiet.

I caught my flight the next morning, and we had a day off. The Pirates were out of town and would be back that night with a day off the next day. I was glad I could rest the leg an extra day and thought maybe Leyland would not need me to pinch hit for a couple of days.

That first night back in uniform felt weird, almost like a prisoner feels after being released. I had been out of the Big Leagues for two years, but now I had worked my way back. It felt like a dream. When I got to the clubhouse, I saw my name in the lineup. That was bitter sweet. I had a strained hamstring, but I had played hurt before; I would get through it.

When I had been in the Big Leagues before, everyone just stretched on their own; now everybody stretched as a team. Then we took batting practice and my swing felt good, and so did the hamstring. I took some fly balls in the outfield and felt I was ready to go. The game started, and in the first inning the Cardinals had a runner at second with one out. There was a base hit to right, and as I started to charge the ball, I felt the hamstring pull. I slowed down, scooped the ball, and made the throw. The runner beat the throw by a half step.

Back in my prime, this was an easy play, but this night the fact that I had lost a step was magnified by my undisclosed injury. I am sure the people that had seen me in my prime were saying, "What has happened to this guy? He was the man with a cannon arm back in the late eighties."

I had finally made it back to the Bigs, and now I was hurt. If I said something to the trainer, I would look like I was making excuses or that I wanted to go on the disabled list. I was way too proud to do that, so I decided I would just play with the injury.

The rest of the night went fine, except for the three strikeouts. My family was watching back home at a restaurant, and when I called home after the game, they wanted to know what happened. They could tell something was not right. "Why did you strike out so much?" Glenn Jr. would ask me later. He was old enough to know when a player did not play well.

I would get one more start later that month and a few pinch hit appearances. The last start would come in San Francisco. Leyland told me the night before the game, and for the first time since I was a rookie, I could not fall asleep. This would be my 1200th game to play in the Big Leagues, and I could not sleep. I would be starting in center field, because Jim was giving Andy Van Slyke an off day.

After the second inning of that game in San Francisco, I was jogging off the field and my heels were hurting so bad that I wanted to cry. No matter how much I hurt, I was not coming out of the game. I scored a hit that inning off Trevor Wilson, no relation, so the pain was bearable. It was funny because when I got that hit, the umpire at second base was Paul Runge, who I had grown to like over the years. He asked me if I wanted the ball. I said no and just laughed.

Later that game, I got hit number 1098: a single up the middle. It would be the last hit of my career. I had one thousand ninety-eight hits, and ninety-eight of them were home runs. That was the ball I should have asked for, but I did not realize at the time that it was all over. Just like the uncertainty of life, you never know when it may be your last time to walk onto the field. I finished the game and did not get to two balls in center, where years ago I could have tracked both of them down easily.

We left that evening for St Louis, and the first game there was on a Monday night. The strangest thoughts were taking place in my mind. As we were stretching as a team, I heard a James Taylor song being played on the loud speakers. The song was saying, "I've seen fire and I've seen rain. I've seen sunny days that I thought would never end."

As I listened to it, something came over me, and a replay of my career began in my head. This thought kept creeping in that was telling me to enjoy the day. I could not shake the inner voice; it was consuming my thoughts.

I remembered Roger Craig telling me when I was a rookie to "play every game like it's your last, because it just might be."

That day I had one of the most enjoyable batting practices of my career. That thought of enjoying this night would not go away, so I listened to it and made it my goal to enjoy that night.

Right before game time, I grabbed a cup of coffee and sat at the end of the bench with the most peaceful feeling I ever felt in a baseball uniform. In the third inning, Van Slyke went for a ball in center, crashing into the wall like he had done a hundred times in his career. Only this time, he was not getting up from the warning track. He had broken his collarbone.

A week before, Jim Leyland had come up to me during batting practice in the outfield and asked me some personal questions. When I had been with the Pirates in 1989, he did this to all the starters and some of the bench players on a regular basis. I think it was Leyland's way of checking guys out. To me, he was the best manager I ever played for because he genuinely cared about you; he wanted to make sure that his horses were not having any problems off the field. So when he asked me that day if I was ok financially, I was taken off guard. I assured him things were great…it was one time I definitely should not have lied.

The truth was that I was going broke when the Astros did not follow through with the contract extension they had promised. To make things worse, when I was out of baseball those two years was when the IRS disallowed the investments my agents made on my behalf. On top of that, my wife Kim was a power shopper and I spent money quickly and efficiently as well.

As fate would have it, Leyland told me to go play centerfield. As I was running on the field, I nodded to Frank Pulley who was the umpire at second base. He was one of very few umpires I liked and had not argued with during my career.

He asked, "Willie, what are you doing?"

"Frank, I'm still trying to figure that out."

"See me when the inning is over."

I thought about what he wanted as I stood out in centerfield. I had been out after games and ended up at the same bars as him over the years, and we had shared some funny stories. So after the inning, I jogged up to him. He walked with me and said, "Willie, if I move to my left, it's an off speed pitch. If I move to my right, it's a fast ball." What was going on? No umpire had ever offered to help me like that before.

Chapter 7

Game number 1201 as a Big Leaguer would be my last. I went to the hotel bar after the game and a young beat writer I scarcely knew asked me if I heard the Pirates were calling up two outfielders: Will Pennyfeather and Ben Shelton. I thought that was weird because we only needed one outfielder to replace Van Slyke who was out for two months; I figured his injury meant I would play more in centerfield.

Then the next morning Leyland called my room and quickly said, "I've got to let you go," then hung up.

The team was designating me for assignment, and I did not receive a real explanation. Neither did I receive any encouragement; no, "Hey, I appreciate the effort" or "You had a good career"; just, "I've got to let you go." Now I was devastated. It happened in the blink of an eye. One day I was patrolling the outfield of Busch Stadium, and the next day I was told I am no longer good enough. Even though that voice in my mind the day before was telling me it was over and to enjoy the moment; I don't think any athlete wants to admit they cannot play anymore. It is tough to achieve something as amazing as being a pro athlete only to realize the dream you had been living is finished.

Later that day, I went to the clubhouse to get my baseball equipment. Roger Wilson, the Pirates' clubhouse manager, had it all packed for me. I only had one coach come over to me and say goodbye, and that was Tommy Sandt. I asked Tommy if Leyland was in his office and he said yes, so I headed in to talk to him before I left the ballpark. Jim was getting dressed and started rambling about how Casey Stengel was falling asleep on the bench late in his career as a manager. Not knowing what to say, I just said thanks and left.

To this day, I am of the opinion that Leyland was (and still is) mad about me going over his head after he had supposedly traded me to the Astros. He has never returned a phone call, and I have tried to get in touch with him several times. Some people just are always right, I know I felt that way about myself for a long time. Jim also said I could wait until the next day's game and fly back to Pittsburgh with the team, but I think he knew me well enough to know I would not take him up on the offer.

That night, for the first time in my adult life, I went and bought a ticket, sat down near the third baseline, and watched the game from the stands. After three innings I had enough. I could not bear to watch anymore, so I went to the airport and caught a flight back to Pittsburgh.

I went to Three Rivers Stadium the next day to get my belongings out of my locker. Then I went upstairs to the front office to get my final check; that is where things grew strange. As I was waiting in the lobby, Ted Simmons passed by me.

"What are you doing here Glenn?" he asked.

"Your manager released me!"

"What?" He looked genuinely flabbergasted.

"Come on Ted, like you didn't know."

"I was just in the hospital with a minor heart attack. That sorry SOB, he released you while I was in the hospital. He must really hate you and this was his opportunity to get rid of you. Will you go back to Buffalo and help Doc try to win that pennant in Triple A?"

"I don't know."

"I'll pay you ten thousand a month on top of your Big League salary."

I perked up at that. "Ok, I'll go help Doc."

Now I was headed back to Triple A. Doc was glad to see me, and we made a valiant run at that pennant. While we were in Iowa, with about a month to go in the season, I was walking across the field for batting practice when I stepped in a small hole in the field and wrenched my back. This was the fourth time I had hurt my back during my career. I attempted to make it through the rest of the road trip. We flew to Louisville, and while we were there I just stayed in bed. I tried to get the muscle spasms to ease up, but it was to no avail.

Since it was obvious my back was not getting better on its own, the trainer had me fly back to Buffalo to see the team doctor. While I was in Buffalo, they put me in the hospital and pumped me full of muscle relaxers and painkillers and took some x-rays. When the pain finally subsided, the doctor informed me that I had three degenerative discs in my lower back and an overlapping disc in my neck that I had since birth. They let me out of the hospital and told me I would not be able to play baseball anymore. The team had two weeks to go in the season and I decided stay there until the end.

Upon release from the hospital, my life would take a dramatic turn for the worse. When I talked with the doctor, he said my back was so bad that I would have to spend the rest of my life on muscle relaxers and painkillers. I did not know that any of the drugs were addictive. I had been an anti-drug person my whole life, other than when I took those steroids back in the winter of 1984. I had tried marijuana once, but did not like the way it made me paranoid and hungry like a wolf. I never tried cocaine or any other illegal drugs because I was too scared because of my dad's heart attack at such a young age and Len Bias' untimely death from drug related causes.

That first pain pill I took gave me a feeling I had never experienced; I relate it to having zero worries while functioning normally. I stayed with the team, watching the games from the stands, and sometimes I felt good enough to get dressed in my uniform and watch the games from the bench. I really wanted to play, but according to the doctor I was now finished as a player. I grew up trusting doctors and never doubted one and I sure never thought a doctor would tell a lie. What would they have to gain in lying to me?

After the season was over, I climbed into my suburban and headed home to Texas. On the way home, I took a few detours. I headed over to Philly first to see some old friends and then to Atlantic City to see other friends and do a little gambling. Next I traveled down the eastern seaboard, just enjoying life. I was still in a little pain at times, but only took the meds as they were prescribed. When I finally got to Texas, Kim was upset that I had not returned straight home.

I had come to grips that I was done with baseball, and I continued taking my meds the way the doctor had instructed, which was making my back feel better. I went to my hometown physician for a second opinion and showed him the x-rays. He agreed that it would be impossible for me to keep playing baseball. Every month I would get my refills, take my meds, relax, and live what I believed was a normal life. Sometimes my back would not hurt for months, but at other times I could not even get out of bed. My back would feel like it was perfect, and then I would bend the wrong way and be laid up in bed for five or six days.

I started playing golf with the same guys I had competed with before returning to baseball, and I was bringing home about seven to eight hundred dollars a day. Sometimes I lost around two hundred, but never two days in a row. These three guys I was playing with would drink while we played, but at that point I refrained from drinking due to my medication. These men were fairly loaded financially and found joy in trying to beat the former pro ball player.

We became close friends and we never had a dispute over how much money was won or lost. We played almost every day during the week and sometimes on weekends. We even traveled and played together in some scramble tournaments. I really liked and respected the men, plus it gave me a competitive outlet to replace baseball.

We all played at about the same skill level, but the one advantage I felt I had over them was my ability to come through under pressure. I learned that we all have a pressure limit when gambling on our abilities. Each one of us brought different skills to the course; one of the guys could not drive the ball very far, but he could putt; another could hit as far as me, but he was an awful putter. The one thing we all had in common was pride. I had individual bets with each one of them, besides our team game, so that I could lose to one guy and still make money.

When I learned about presses, I found I could make a lot of money if I was up. I would try to get up early on the high roller guy because he was a big drinker. He could press as much as he wanted because he had the money and was not afraid to risk it when he was drinking. All of the guys had a good amount of money, but two of them were not alcoholics and were wise in their gambling. Sometimes when I had won three days in a row, I would miss a putt on purpose to make them feel good. I really liked those two, and I even really liked the third guy who had the drinking problem, though not enough to let him win.

Sometimes they all beat me, because they were better than me those specific days, but after the first couple of weeks

I began to hit the ball long and straight. It helped their cause that they were also betting against each other, so even if they lost to me, they made some of the cash back off of each other. If I made seven hundred off the three of them, and one of them beat the other two, he also made money that day. One time the alcoholic guy was really drunk and bet me one of his motorcycles against my golf cart. I really enjoyed riding that Ninja around my neighborhood. Although, I was scared to ride it on the highway and never did take it out.

This went on for about a year and a half. One of the guys had a son about the same age as my oldest, and we became great friends. I would have to say he and I came close to breaking even with each other when it came to our golf games. He was the one who could putt well under pressure.

Sometimes I forgot to take my meds, and it was no big deal. I did not know anything about these medications, so sometimes I would go a week without taking them, feeling like I did not need them. Sometimes I would not even get them refilled when I was out unless my back started to hurt. Then other times I felt like someone was cutting my spine in half, and I would almost fall over. I would get the meds, begin taking them, and start to feel normal again in a week or two.

After the 1994 baseball season, I was at home and received a phone call from Bob Boone; he was the manager of the Kansas City Royals. He said that he wanted me to come to spring training for the 1995 season and try to make the club as a right-handed pinch hitter off the bench. I told him I had not played since '93, and he said, "That's ok, I think you can help us."

The next week I got a call from Del Unser of the Phillies, and he said he had the dreaded job of trying to find replacement players, since the Big Leaguers were on strike. I had read a little about it and told him I could not play because I was part of the union and they had done so much for me. I did not feel it would be right to be a replacement player. He then offered me sixty thousand just to come to spring training. I told him I could not do it and he said he understood. After receiving the call from Unser, I called Bob Boone back.

"You're not offering me to be a replacement player are you?"

He assured me, "Absolutely not. I don't think the strike will last into spring training. I will pay you $750,000 if you make the team out of spring training and $10,000 a month for the time you spent in Triple A." So he sent me a contract, and my good golfing buddy and I started working out.

Boy was I out of shape. But I worked hard and showed up to spring training ready to go. When I got there, however, the strike was still active, so they told the players that had contracts to just work out with the Triple A team until the strike broke. They were using replacement players at the spring training stadium. Then after about two weeks, the farm director had a meeting with us and said that if we did not cross the picket line, we would be kicked out of spring training. So rather than cross the picket line, I decided to spend a week going to the beach, Sea World, and the amusement parks, since my family had come down to visit me.

The strike broke and instead of going to the stadium, I was told to drive to Omaha and start the season with the Triple A team. As I was driving there, I received a phone call on my car phone from the Triple A manager, Mike Jirschele, informing me that I had been released. He said he was sorry, and that he had been told to wait until I reached Omaha to tell me. He said he did not want to wait because he had heard of my reputation as a loose cannon at times, and he did not want me to kill him or just break him in two pieces. I told him he made the right decision.

As I was driving through Henrietta, Oklahoma, hometown of Troy Aikman, according to the billboard, I made a u-turn and called the Player's Association. I was hot because Bob Boone had lied to me. How could I be so stupid as to think a team would really need me at the age of 36? The Player's Association set up a spring training with all expenses paid for the guys this was happening to.

I drove home and caught a flight to Miami as they had us working out in Homestead, Florida. No coaches were present, just two really cute workout girls leading us in stretching. Then we would have an inter-squad game and could be done and at Doral country club by one p.m. Other players who joined me in Homestead were: Andy Van Slyke, Howard Johnson, Robin Ventura, Jay Howell, Lloyd McClendon, and about twenty-five others. The best part about being there was the golf at Doral because we played the blue monster free of charge every day. I say free of charge, but we signed a lot of autographs. Some guys were signed out of that special training camp onto Major League rosters, but I was one of the ones who did not get a contract.

I headed back home pissed at Bob Boone and sad that I did not get another chance to continue my career. I respected Del Unser; at least he had told me the truth, but for Boone to just flat out lie, was a shame to the game of baseball. While I was down in Doral, I must have called Bill Giles, the owner of the Phillies, at least five times, asking for a chance to come to their camp. It was to no avail; when the camp was over, so was my career as a baseball player.

I settled back into my routine living in Houston and started playing golf again. I had been informed of the collusion results; that the owners had been found guilty and were ordered to pay the Player's Association millions of dollars. There had never been any formula of how to divide up this kind of money for this many former and current ballplayers. They had to figure out a way to try to satisfy everyone that felt they had a claim. Over the next eight years I was told I would receive a total amount of nearly $400,000.

Although a nice sum of money, it was once again a far cry from what my agents said I would be receiving from collusion. If a player was not in agreement with the Players Association's decision, they could take it to an independent arbitrator. My agents told me my first three checks would be for $27,500, and we did not need to object to it since they were informed that my final two checks would be $250,000 because those were the years I had really been cheated. Of course they were right on the first three checks but they missed the mark on the final two checks by $100,000 each.

I insisted that I wanted to arbitrate, but they advised against it. I finally stood up to my so-called agents and said, "If you won't arbitrate it for me, I will find someone who will." They took my case, though they did not take it seriously. They told me the flight to be on so we could discuss my case while flying to Los Angeles. Then it turned out they had taken a different flight. During my hearing, my so-called agents, whom I had trusted early in my career, hardly said a word on my behalf. I quickly realized their argument on my behalf was weak and I ended up doing most of the talking on my own defense.

The strange part was that I was in a conference room in Los Angeles, California, making an argument against the very union I had been a part of my entire baseball career. This was the same union that I had refused to cross the picket line against in 1995 when being offered $60,000 dollars. I was being represented by the very guys that had threatened me when I tried to fire them in 1991. They were big name agents that loved their press clippings. Sitting there, I knew that no one in that room could care less whether I won the case or was out a large sum of money.

I could not do anything for these agents anymore and I knew I could not support nor help the union anymore. Agents are not necessary as a player in Major League Baseball. The owners of a Major League Baseball team don't care about you unless you are performing. Greed is everywhere in pro baseball. Egos are huge; including the egos of front office staff, agents, coaches, and players. Pro Baseball was an evil environment, full of egos and deception.

The mindset in baseball is characterized by the line in the movie *Remember the Titans,* when a character says "I'm going to get mine." That is the attitude you better have because when your career is over, they sure won't need you or send you a Christmas card.

That would be the last time I would speak to the Hendricks brothers, who were my best friends when I was an up-and-coming rookie. These were the same guys that had taken out ten term life insurance policies on me from their other brother. When all was said and done with the disbursement of the collusion money, the same big name players got the bulk of it, we lesser names received much less… imagine that!

A word of advice to young players: Do not fall into the trap of thinking you have to have an agent. Many players assume when they prepare to enter a pro sport that they are required to have an agent. My advice is: Trust no one when it comes to your money, surround yourself with people who care about you more than your money, and realize that agents talk, and if you make them mad they will try to get even with you. At least if you manage your career yourself and you are broke when it is over, you can only blame yourself.

It was time to find a real job, since the gas station I had purchased was losing money every year, and my agents had been putting money in it without informing me. I was forced to sell it and look for a different way to earn income.

When I asked my agents for all documentation from my career, they refused to provide paperwork. When I spoke with their assistant, who I thought was a strong Christian, she turned into a wolf, saying that sometimes in investing things just don't work out as you plan. When I told her I felt that I was misrepresented by her bosses, she sounded like a sailor just home from a long tour of duty as she explained her opinion of me in numerous colorful words.

Chapter 8

Since being away from baseball as a player, I have held several different jobs. I have sold cars, worked in the freight forwarding industry, dabbled in multi-level marketing, and even worked for a hotshot company. I remember several deliveries I had to make to the new stadium the Astros were building; that was a humbling realization that my dream job had turned into a distant memory.

I worked one year for a company called Comcast Sports as a baseball analyst for Phillies pre- and post-game shows. I also did this at Fox Sports in Houston for Astros post-game shows. Neither of those jobs resulted in me being asked to return for a second season, and I never received feedback as to what was missing in my skills.

I managed four years of Minor League Baseball, with three of those years ending in the championship series.

I had always disliked umpires in general. I hardly ever got on an umpire because he was a bad umpire. When an umpire wanted to show me that they were in control of the game or acted cocky in anyway, I was going to show them up by making them feel stupid. I was also developing severe anger problems, which was manifested one night when I got so mad that I went to kick dirt on an umpire. He was awful and would purposely screw a guy or two just because he had the authority to affect the game. When I kicked at the dirt, my foot slipped across the top and I nailed the umpire's shin guard.

One night, while managing the Chillicothe team on a road trip, an umpire tried messing over my players. At one point, he took a home run away from one of my favorite players, John "Rambo" Ramistella. Rambo hit a mammoth home run down the leftfield line that was lifted so high that God could have caught it, but this umpire called it a foul ball.

I normally could not see a ball hit down the line like that when I was in the third base dugout, but because of the way this ball was hit, I had time to take three steps toward the field before it cleared the fence. You know a ball is hit high and far when the hitter is jogging to first and gets there before the umpire makes a call. The ump waited for the ball to land, which took twenty seconds, then he looked at me and called it foul. I lost it and told him about his family and how his life would be miserable the rest of the year. He ejected me from the game.

I went to my pitching coach, James Frisbee, and told him, "On the next hitter, I don't care where the first pitch is, you get thrown out, too." Our super-nice-guy coach was not able to make the trip, so I knew I could make this umpire's life miserable. Before I even got to the clubhouse, my coach was already gone. He had a temper also and playing off my lead he took his chewing tobacco/gum mixture out of his mouth and threw it in the stands.

Now I had no coach to coach the game because we had both been kicked out. What I did have was a bunch of guys that would run through a wall for me because they knew I would stick up for them and never embarrass them. I told one of my pitchers to turn the boys loose, and if there was a close call and they did not get thrown out, I would release them the next day. Needless to say, we lost that game, and the umpire had a tough night.

As I worked as a manager, I was also becoming a loner. I never went out after a single game. I never drank because I was smart enough to know you do not mix a prescription drug with alcohol. I drove my own vehicle to all the games, even on the road. That was mainly so the players could use it to go out after road games. I would study stats on the opposing teams constantly. I stayed in my hotel room or apartment until it was time to go to the park. I only felt I was there for one thing, and that was to win. I had an owner I could never get in touch with by phone. The one thing that he was adamant about was that I let him know about a trade before I made it.

One time, I literally tried to call the owner ten times before a trade. The reason was because I was about to trade the most popular player on our team. We had just finished the first half of the season, and I had seen all the other teams. I knew we were not a very good team, but we had a decent nucleus. The player I needed to trade was going to be my bait in order to get the two players I felt we needed to make a run in the second half. I was even going to send the player's best friend with him, because I know what it's like to be traded and not know anyone on your new team. I felt comfortable sending his best friend as well because the friend could only hit a fastball in the mid eighties and could not touch a breaking ball. I did not have enough time to work with him and win a championship.

Naturally, the owner does not return my calls, and I have the other team's manager ready to pull the trigger because his team had gone south and he had attitude problems with the two guys I wanted. Bad attitudes are easy to fix if you know the player's background. A change of scenery for a bad attitude can make a world of difference.

I proceeded ahead and traded the popular guy first and got a Latin second baseman and a feisty centerfielder with Big League speed. Both are switch hitters. The second baseman could be a problem if you did not understand Latin players; I did, so I told him, "If you want to take batting practice that's fine. If you don't that's fine too. You let me know what you need, or if anything is bothering you, and I will fix it. In return, I need you to get me to the championship."

"Ok, Poppy."

And just like that, I never had a problem with Juan Downing.

The center fielder, Steve Martin, became one of my favorites because he was a free spirit but played as hard as anyone who ever played the game. He ran out every ground ball like he could beat it. That is a rarity in Indy ball and even in the Big Leagues now with all the big money being paid. We made the playoffs and the championship series. Without those two young men, we would not have made it to the series.

Then we did it again the next year, although my center fielder had lost his bat and then his confidence. I stayed with him as long as I felt I could because of what he had done for us the year before, but then I had to release him. That same night, he was in a car accident and was killed. I was called at three in the morning and went to the hospital, identified the body, prayed over him, and wept. He comes to my mind a lot these days. I felt sorry for his family but knew he was saved when his mom told me at the funeral. I now think of how lucky he was to not have to be away from the game he loved so much before getting the call to Heaven.

I was not asked back the next year to manage.

Since it seemed, at least for the moment, the doors to manage were closed, I started an advisory service for high school baseball players and also branched into football to help promote athletes. I have seen that there is still a need for promotion of high school athletes, just as it was needed when I was coming out of high school.

How does a kid go from no scholarships out of high school to a first round draft pick after three years of college? Did he become that much better in three years, or did he get missed by every school on the planet as well as by all Major League organizations? It baffles me to this day. I know college baseball budgets are small, but pro budgets are huge. That is why I promote the kids that are not getting the exposure that they should. Most parents do not understand the system and really need help.

Another benefit of coming home was more time with my youngest son, Andy, who was a freshman in high school and a pretty good athlete. . I would spend the next year watching him play high school football and baseball. Even though he was a freshman, he made the varsity team in both sports. I felt he should have played freshman football instead of being on the varsity team. His coach and I had gone to college together, so I did not know Andy was on the team because of our relationship or because the coach really needed him. I would find out later it was because Andy was already over two hundred pounds, so they felt they could use him on defense.

In baseball, I thought there was no way he could hit varsity pitching. I knew he could handle the outfield because of his athleticism, but he would prove me wrong by hitting over .400 as a freshman in baseball while making some decent plays on defense in football.

His freshman year, during a football game against the Woodlands High School, we had a moment I will never forget. He started the first half and I could tell from the stands he was playing scared. The Woodlands was a powerhouse team every year. During half time, I was trying to think of something to say to motivate him. I went on the field and stood near the blowup tunnel the players run through to come onto the field. He ran over to me when he saw me, and I could see fear in his eyes. So, like most dads, I said something encouraging.

"Son," I said as I grabbed him by the jersey and jerked him to my face, "You're embarrassing your family. If you don't start making plays, I will come on this field and take that uniform off of you myself." I know it sounds cruel. I would think the same thing, but what happened later excused what I said. I picked him up from the school after the game and we had a talk.

"Son, are you scared?" I asked him.

"Yes, sir."

"You want to get rid of that fear?"

"Yes, sir,"

"When we get home and you get something to eat, meet me in your bedroom." We met in his bedroom and I brought my Bible. I started to share with him for the first time about what Jesus did for us. I don't remember word for word what I said, but that night my youngest son accepted Jesus as Lord and Savior. A few months later, he was baptized.

While Andy was excelling on the sports field, my middle son, Lance, was at a junior college. At least that is what we were led to believe. Lance was actually in the middle of a devastating drug addiction. By that point so was I. I had been taking pain killers as prescribed by my doctor with absolutely no knowledge of their after effects for over eleven years. I was watching *60 Minutes* one Sunday night, and they were talking about prescription painkillers while showing stories of those who had become addicted to them. My world was about to change.

After watching the program I became scared. They had said the painkillers were a powerfully addictive opiate. I remember the hosts and guests talking about how tough it was for people to stop taking them because of the painful withdrawals that came when trying to stop. That next day, I went to my doctor and was enraged that he had never warned me of the addictive nature of the drugs he had given me so many years ago. I asked, "Why didn't you tell me this drug was addicting?"

"Yes they can be addicting," he said trying to calm me down, "but your back is so mangled that you need them."

I could not come to terms with being a drug addict. So I decided I would try to quit before my life was characterized by being addicted to pain pills. That was where the struggle began to shape my life. I started counting how many I had left, and when my bottle would start getting low, I would start to panic. It was a panic accompanied by a fear of what would happen if I did not take them. I continued this process for four years, taking as many as twenty pills in one day on a few occasions. I felt trapped. I could not tell my wife... I could not tell anyone. I thought I was against drugs and that there was no way this could happen to me.

I was able to bring myself down to seven pills on an average day. I never bought them on the street, but I did have a friend that was on them. If he or I ran out early, one of us would go to a clinic and act like we were in severe pain. The drug became my reason for getting out of bed. I would spend the next four years trying to get off those pills. I never even considered a rehab facility because that meant telling my wife I had a problem and my kids finding out. I was so ashamed and helpless.

Then I found out my middle son Lance was hooked on them as well. If I ran out, I got them from him. He told me he was getting them from a doctor, so in my mind it was okay if we shared since we were both prescribed these drugs. What an idiot I was to believe that story. If he ran out, I would give him some of mine because I knew what the withdrawals were like. He was taking his addiction to a whole different level; a level that makes me wonder how he is alive today.

Lance and I developed a close relationship because we both had to keep a secret from his mother and his two brothers. The only difference between us was that he was taking Somas with the painkillers during the day, and I was taking a sleep aid at night. At one point, I remember trying to help him get off the pills, while I was still on them. It is hard to help someone or impact someone's life when you are in despair and addiction as well.

One Sunday in January of 2008, I went to a local church by myself, and the preacher was preaching from the Book of Revelation in the Bible. I thought that where he was reading from sounded familiar, but I had never read The Bible at any length. I was the guy that was always saying I could not understand The Bible. I was saved at sixteen through a now Hollywood actor and producer named Alan Stepp. Alan had read some of the book of Revelation to me and invited me to a revival at the Methodist church in Channelview. That was all I needed and wanted from God.

I had been to church some when my sons were little, and we had been visiting a mega-church in the Houston area for about eight years on a very inconsistent basis. After church, I would usually say something like, "I could have done a better job than that preacher."

One of my biggest questions about that church was wondering why they were always asking for money. My mother-in-law Thel and I had several discussions over the years about tithing, but I would not listen to her. During the service, I would be typically thinking about my golf game after church rather than being engaged with what was being said.

That Sunday evening, after I attended the local church, I was on the phone with a current Houston Astros player because we had been discussing a business venture. The conversation got ugly when I told him I would not be going through with the deal we had made. It pissed him off, and he started to yell through the phone. It disturbed me so much I clicked the off button and threw the phone down. Then I picked up my Bible and began to read.

I had a lot going on in my life besides trying to get off those pills. As mentioned before, I had started a business trying to help high school baseball players get scholarships. My wife had been an interior decorator since I retired from baseball. She was great at it and found it was something she loved. In my free time I was playing golf with some new friends I had met in the area where we had moved for my youngest son's high school years. We moved there, because the coach and I had gone to college together. He had us come out to one of his practices and had Andy throw with his varsity players while still just an eighth grader at another school. This is illegal in Texas high school football, but it is done frequently.

My wife Kim would watch Joyce Meyer Ministries on television every morning. I was always telling her to beware of false prophets. I have no idea why I would say that about Joyce Meyer. Kim would leave in the mornings, and I would turn the TV channel to country music videos. Then I would dabble on the Internet, take a shower, and go play golf. In the evenings I would always go watch high school baseball games. All the while, I would be taking about seven of my pain pills throughout the day. I was crippled by the fear of not taking them, but was eaten up by anxiety from taking them as well. I worried about everything.

I was also consumed with the fear of not having enough money. My wife was the kind of person that was always encouraging and positive, but I was the total opposite. Since baseball was over, I was the negative, glass-half-empty guy. I wanted my way; that's how it would be, and no one could convince me otherwise.

I started to receive my retirement income around that time. During the days that I did not go play golf or have to be at a baseball game, I was wracked with bitterness toward baseball. I had managed four years and been to the championship series three times, but no one wanted to hire me. I could not get a Major League organization to hire me as a coach. I was a miserable person. The only thing I had to look forward to was my son Andy's high school football games.

I did not want him to play baseball, just as I had never wanted my other sons to play baseball. I did not want my kids to think they had to live up to being a Major League player like their dad. Plus, I knew how hard the game could be and the pressures that came with it, and I did not want them to have to face what I experienced. In spite of my hope that none of them would play baseball, Andy decided to play baseball and football. So I would go to the games. I never told him anything negative about the game or how he played it, but instead tried to encourage him about how great he was and that he was better than me at that age. I also never told him I wished he was not playing.

On that Sunday, January 8th, when I picked up my Bible it looked brand new. It was a wedding gift from my mother-in-law Thel from 1980, and I was not surprised it looked so new because I had never really had much desire to read it. I cracked open the pages, and it flipped to Jeremiah 29:11 which reads, "'For I know the plans that I have for you,' declares the LORD, 'plans for welfare and not for calamity to give you a future and a hope.'"

I put The Bible down and went to my closet. As I got down on my knees, I was thinking about how bad things had turned out in my life. At times it honestly seemed like no one cared. I was trapped in this addiction that I could not tell anyone about, and I was all alone trying to conquer all these fears. Why did I make it to the Big Leagues and to an All-star game only to gradually decline to the point of not being able to find a job in the league? As all these thoughts began to flood my mind, I began to pray out loud.

"God, I need you. I don't know anything except baseball, and I want you to take over my life. Please help me. I cannot give up these pills without your help. I surrender all to you." Then I got up and went to bed.

Up until that night, I really only knew one verse in The Bible, which was John 3:16. I only knew that one because it can be seen at almost every sporting event on TV. When Alan Stepp invited me to that revival when I was sixteen, I accepted Jesus as Lord and Savior. My problem was not that I did not believe; it's just that I thought my salvation gave me a free pass to sin or, that I could sin as much as I wanted and simply ask for forgiveness. I saw Jesus as a way to live my life as sinfully as I wanted but still not have to worry about life after death. And while it is true upon salvation God forgives us of all of our sins, it is not a license to sin just so God's grace can cover it. That kind of thinking perverts and takes advantage of the beautiful gift of grace that God gives us.

I also did not realize the benefits of reading The Bible and did not understand that being a Christian was more than belief; it was about having an actual relationship with Jesus. All my life, when I was playing baseball or managing, I would put the radio on to listen to a preacher on Sundays and thought that was enough…oh, how little I knew back then.

I never hesitated to tell people that I was a Christian when I was playing in the Majors, but I rarely went to church or chapel. I looked at the guys that went to chapel as weak ball players. I did not want to associate with them. How could anyone really be a Christian while in the Big Leagues while surrounded by all the women and whiskey? I remember Tom Foley and Milt Thompson always asking me to come to chapel, and I would actually make fun of them behind their backs. I really just wanted to continue being a Big Leaguer and enjoy everything that went with it. I did not want to be mister goody two-shoes. There was no fun in that, and I wanted to be center of attention in all the wrong places and for all the wrong reasons. I thought I was going to die young like my dad, so I was going to enjoy the Big League life while it lasted. The times I did attend chapel, I would make jokes about the stories by asking questions like," Did Jesus feed the 5,000 with bass or catfish?"

Now I found myself at this crossroads of life realizing how little I knew about what really mattered. In my arrogance I thought I knew so much.

Chapter 9

W hile lying in bed, I started to repeat "*The Lord's Prayer*." After repeating it many times, I sat up in bed when I got stuck on "thy will be done." I somehow realized for the first time that this meant God's will be done; not my will, but His will. Then it happened, for the first time in my life, I heard God's voice. It was not an audible voice, but a voice that came from inside of me. It was clearer than any voice I have ever heard in my life. Speaking to me, God said, "You have been anointed. Get ready for the miracle and I will restore your teeth."

At the time, I did not know what the word anointed meant; it was a churchy sounding word that was foreign to me. In trying to decipher this Godly message, I figured the miracle meant Jesus was coming again really soon. Restore your teeth? This part threw me for a loop as I had no clue what God meant by the proclamation, though the pain pills had taken a toll on my teeth.

Right after hearing this message from God, I turned and looked at my wife and saw small wings on her back. I know that this sounds like I was having some kind of drug-related withdrawal, but I must admit I was still taking the painkillers. I had not changed a thing, and in the moment there was not even a second that I entertained the thought that I was having drug illusions or withdrawals. I knew this was divine intervention, but since I was new to this God stuff, I was thoroughly confused. God continued to speak to me through visions as I sat up wide awake in my bed.

The next vision was of my oldest son, Glenn Jr., appearing at the end of my bed. He looked strong and confident. He exemplified everything we wanted in our sons. Then he faded away and there was the image of my middle son, Lance, standing there. He looked cold and was shivering. I felt such a depth of sorrow for him as I watched him shake and shiver. It was the third vision that deeply bothered me. It was my youngest son, Andy, standing there, and I felt a deep sorrow and could feel my wife's pain for him as well. It was as if something bad would happen to him.

It scared me so much that I got out of bed, went to his bedroom, got on my knees, placed my hand on him, and began to pray. Without waking him up, I finished my prayer. Then I went to Lance's room and did the same thing, praying from the depths of my soul for him. I had never prayed that fervently before in my entire life. While praying over Lance, I asked God to give me Lance's drug withdrawals; I actually said, "Father, if your son could die on the cross for me, then this is the least I can do for my son."

Then I walked into the hall bathroom and was staring at the mirror. Looking into the mirror, it felt as if something was happening inside of me. I said to the mirror, "No, you're not making me into you," speaking of Jesus. Why was I feeling and acting like this? I went to the living room and sat on the couch. While sitting there, I was having so many thoughts about someone dying. I thought about every member in my family, and then it hit me.

This must be the way we all die. You have this visit from God, and this is how He prepares you for Heaven. After thinking about all my family members that might be about to die, I thought about me as being the one who was going to die. When I had that thought, there was an overwhelming feeling of peace if that was the way my life was going to end.

Then I looked up at a painting that had been over the fireplace since we moved into the house. I noticed for the first time that it was a painting of a cross. The frame was five feet by five feet, and the cross in the frame stretched from top to bottom. It was twelve inches wide from top to bottom. While seeing this, I looked at the top of the cross, and this is when I started to cry. At the top of the cross was Jesus' face. As I was crying, I was holding a blanket and a football; my wife, Kim, had gotten out of bed and had come to check on me with a worried look.

"Glenn… Are you okay?"

"I don't know, but I think God is about to take me home."

She tried to comfort me, and then she went back to bed. I was getting tired now too, and not too long after Kim went back to sleep, I went back to bed as well.

The next morning, while Kim and I were having coffee, I was trying to explain everything that had happened that night. I could not stop crying and was telling her the devil was in the bottle of pain pills. I was then trying to tell her all that had happened, but when I would try to speak, it was as if I was dry heaving. As I would dry heave, I would confess a sin to her. I was extremely upset and had no idea why all of this had happened to me. She was very concerned about me.

She had work to do that day, and I had to be in Ft. Worth that evening. So I took a shower, got dressed, went to the pharmacy and got my prescription, and headed to Ft. Worth. A friend of mine named Lavell Morgan drove because I wanted to read my Bible. I read for the entire drive. When we arrived, we sat up our booth at the convention center and then to our hotel. While at my hotel, I could not stop watching ministers on TV. Then I hit my knees, said my prayers, and went to bed.

When we were walking into the convention center the next day, I felt like I was drunk. I was so wobbly that I had to hold onto the railing. Then while at our booth, I was extremely nice to people when they would come by. Now I do not mean I was ever a mean person to people, but I had never in my life been that nice. When I sat down and looked up at the lights, it felt like they were swaying. I could not focus. I was not overly worried, but I must admit I was a little concerned.

When the day was over, I went back to my room and watched TV preachers, even Catholic priests. It did not matter; I had to feel something inside of me. I would have to think since my friend Lavell had played for me when I managed, he must have thought his former skipper was losing it. When I returned from the trip, I decided to get rid of the pills. I finished the prescription I had and kept reading The Bible. The more I read, the more I understood and wanted to read. I continued to watch different ministers on the television, though I had narrowed them down to about three and as well as the *700 Club*.

On Sundays, I started going to the church that I had been visiting the past eight or nine years. I was also starting to hear several country songs that were talking about faith. I had even come to the point of keeping my truck radio on a Christian station. Money was thin, so thin that I had to turn in one of my cars to the bank. I remember praying that night over that vehicle. My nephew Carey Poarch Jr. watched as I asked that the Lord would use it to bless and protect whoever got the car. I had no idea why my behavior had become so different.

Over the next few weeks I could not stop reading The Bible and I started seeing things differently. On February the

12th, I woke up, took a shower and grabbed my checkbook. I needed to go to my bank to cash a check because it was my wife's birthday. As I was driving, I came upon a bridge, and at the beginning of it I felt my throat get scratchy. As I got to the top of the bridge, I could not swallow my saliva. I began to panic, and I saw a sign that said "Donut Shop." I raced into that parking lot and ran in the shop.

There was an Asian man sitting there, and I asked him for a cup of water. He casually walked to the back while I tried to remain calm. Then he emerged with a large cup of water. I reached into my pocket and found all I had on me was a quarter. So I pulled the quarter out of my pocket and placed it on his counter as I began to gulp down the water. Thankfully, the water was working as I started to feel better.

As I got back to my truck I noticed I had no gas in the tank, and unfortunately I only had my checkbook with me. I started up my truck and headed back across that bridge. As I was driving in the direction I had just come from, I knew I was not going back to the house. I still did not know where I was going though.

I came to the intersection where a left turn would take me home, but I noticed my water was low. I started to get scared again, so I turned right. This was the way to the church, and it was then I knew God wanted me to go there. I am guessing that this was my fourth or fifth day off of the pills, and I hadn't had any withdrawals at all. At least, not the withdrawals they say you will have when you stop taking pills as addictive as the ones I had been on for one and a half decades.

As I walked into the church, I was greeted by a nice lady named Mary Ellen who asked. "May I help you?"

"I think you know why I'm here."

"Can I get a minister to pray with you?"

"Sure."

All the time I was thinking that I would finally meet the head pastor of this church and tell him whatever God wanted him to hear using me as his mouthpiece. Well, to no surprise, a pinch-hit pastor named Steve was who I met. He asked if we could go to some room so I could tell him what was going on and we could pray.

I tried to say, "My name is Glenn Wilson, and I used to play for the Astros."

What actually came out of my mouth, as I hit my knees and my eyes flooded with tears was "I'm the guy after the service who always says 'Why are y'all always asking for money?'" I confessed some more sins without trying and finally was able to stop crying. Pastor Steve prayed with me, and I was on my way. Mary Ellen gave me another full cup of water and I felt I was good to go, so I headed out of the church.

Maybe I was in the beginning stages of drug withdrawals, or maybe I was having a nervous breakdown, but I can only tell you what I saw and what happened next in my journey. It was an overcast day, and as I started for my truck, I noticed a large black cloud in the sky. It was about one hundred feet above the ground on the other side of my truck. The closer I got to my truck, the closer the lightning filled cloud seemed to get to the truck as well. The lightning bolts were violent and I knew we were going to meet. My great grandfather had been struck by lightning many years ago, so I jumped in my truck as fast as I could since I was not interested in suffering the same fate.

At this point, I was sure I was going to die. This idea of impending death had been a theme in my life since that night on January the 8th. I backed out of the parking spot and proceeded to head home. I noticed that the song on the radio was saying let it pour down like rain and something about sins being washed away. Then I noticed it kept getting louder, and I was not touching the volume. I was really scared now, so I called my wife on the cell phone in a panic and told her I have always loved her and that I was about to die.

It started raining so hard that it looked like I was driving on a lake. As I went through an intersection, I kept thinking that a car was about to broadside me. I asked God to let me make it home one more time to hug and kiss my wife goodbye.

When I finally pulled in my driveway, I got out of the truck and let the rain fall on me. I started yelling at God that I knew He was real; that He was really, really, real. Drenched from the rain, I walked into the house as a man on a mission. I can remember a few things that happened next, but keep in mind I know and have known I was going to die. The things I can remember are: believing that was possibly my last moment with my family; preaching to my wife and Lance, holding The Bible in the air, seeing lighting strike outside and hearing the impounding thunder. I remember telling my wife and son to hold my hands and feel God's power. I remember thinking that either my son was going to shoot me or I would have to shoot him, though I knew that shooting him was not an option, so he would have to shoot me.

The reason I was thinking these things is that I was remembering what Jesus said about how he did not come to bring peace on earth, but to bring a son against a father and a daughter against a mother-in-law. Looking back, I can see that there was a war going on for my soul. The devil was trying to use scripture to deceive me. I remember talking on the phone to my father-in-law Bill and thinking that it was my real dad that had died when I was a kid.

I guess you could say my wife was more than a little scared by now. She had called my oldest son and Mike Zatopek, a childhood friend and wonderfully godly man, who were on their way to our house. Mike had already called Houston Methodist Hospital to let them know we would be coming. Then out of nowhere came a pain in my chest like a car was sitting on it. I grew increasingly exhausted and I remember thinking, "Thank God, I am finally going to get to die." It had been a tough day, and as I fell back onto the couch in exhaustion, I took several last looks at my dad's picture and at the clock.

Since my dad died of a heart attack, I always wanted to know what it felt like, and for some reason I always wanted to know what time he had died as well. My face hit the couch pillow and I was ready, but God wasn't ready for me.

As I buried my face in the pillow, I felt God say, "I am sick and tired of you only giving me bits and pieces of your heart, so I am taking this one and giving you a brand new one."

I was not down more than thirty seconds according to my wife, but to me it felt like thirty minutes. When I sat up I felt fine, all the exhaustion, and chest pressure had been lifted from me.

I could hear and see my oldest son Glenn Jr., and he was saying, "Put your right foot in the shoe, then the left."

I saw my childhood friend Mike there, and all I could remember was asking them how I died. Was it the cigarettes or the pain pills? They proceeded to load me into my son's truck and race me to the Methodist Hospital. During the drive, I began to realize that my vision was starting to blur.

When we arrived, I remember asking if it was a mental hospital or a regular hospital. I was told it took seven people to strap me down to a gurney. I do not remember that, but I do remember them taking me into what I thought was an operating room. I could see the operating light, and I remember having seven nurses in there with me. They would step up to the end of my bed one at a time, and I would start confessing sins to them.

Then one of the most surreal moments of my life began as I felt myself leave my body. I was now standing in front of what I knew was Heaven's gate. The only bad part of this vision was that Hell was right beside it in my view. As I looked at Heaven, it was beautiful and pearly white, a color like nothing I had ever seen before on Earth. The warmth and peace I felt when I looked toward Heaven was beyond any comfort I had ever experienced. Then I looked to my left a little and saw hell. It was long and black, and had a feeling so awful that nothing I can say would describe the terror that I felt. I saw puffs of smoke coming from a long black lake covered in fire. I could hear the distant sound of people screaming for help. I would look at one and then the other, and I kept thinking that I could not wait to go into Heaven.

Then I had a thought that bothers me to this day. I realized I did not know which one I was going to, and at that moment I was thrust back to reality in my body on that table. My right hand was stretched out in the air. My eyes were closed, and I could hear this voice yelling over and over, "You trust me! Don't you?"

I opened my eyes and saw it was Glenn Jr. I calmly said, "Well of course I trust you Glenn, you're my son."

In that moment, I knew I had been given a second chance. My wife told me that the doctors were telling her I was going through drug withdrawals. I may have been, but I do not understand why all of a sudden I had a feeling of life transformation ten times the amount of when I got saved in that Methodist church at the age of sixteen. The only thing the doctors wanted to know was where all of this spiritual stuff was coming from as it was far removed from who I had been in the past. They said I was singing, "Jesus Loves Me," which was funny because I did not know I knew that song.

They kept me in the hospital for six nights to run all kinds of tests. They said at night I would go to the other patient's rooms and read The Bible. I do not remember any of that, but I do remember having my Bible with me to read. That was practically all I did to pass the time in the hospital. They completed all the tests they could do on my brain, heart, and liver. They also did a lot of blood work before saying that I had checked out perfect…imagine that. I was released from the hospital with a clean bill of health.

The next seven months would be the most exciting time in my life. Some of the things are bizarre, to say the least. One of the first things I noticed was when talking to someone; I would talk about sin in the past tense. My middle son, Lance, would point this out to me, and I would apologize and say, "That's right, we are all still sinners."

Many times I would pick up my Bible and just flip it open. Several times it would land on the same page as if

God had specific messages he wanted me to remember in that time of change in my life. Also, when I read the Word, I understood it perfectly and shared my experience with anyone who would listen, but mostly my wife Kim. I felt this urgency to call everyone that I felt I had wronged and ask for their forgiveness. I began to constantly call my oldest brother, Johnie, and we reconciled. We spent some time together, even though he lived in Mississippi.

I carried my Bible everywhere; I had to have it beside me. For the longest time, I was trying to figure out if I was a prophet, a faith healer, or a disciple. I realized, through scripture, that I am just a child of God that had strayed way off the path. I had strayed so far that God had to zap me, as I call it; he zapped me back on course. He put me on the narrow path; the path that led me to my true home. I knew for sure one day I was headed home, and I knew without a doubt that now that eternal home would be Heaven.

Chapter 10

As I write this, I have no idea where God is taking me. What I have learned is God can do what he wants and when he wants to do it. I will just trust Him and seek His kingdom, because he created you and me, and all things work together for good to those who love Him.

My whole life had been about me and what I wanted to accomplish. I had made it to the Big Leagues assumedly on my own power. I was taught if someone treated me wrong, get even with them. My life was characterized by the motto, "I, ME, and MINE."

Life was about winning, not being weak or humble. I coached to win at all costs, even in peewee football where I wanted my players to know I was tough and mean. If you ticked me off, I would show you, or if a parent tried to tell me what to do, I would prove who was the alpha leader. I was Glenn Wilson, former Big Leaguer and you better watch out. Do not get on my bad side, or you would pay dearly. I was always right and held grudges better than almost anyone.

That was my life. God was a mythical figure that was real, but I had never heard of him communicating with anyone. He definitely had no influence on the direction of my life. My plans never included being a preacher. What would He need with me anyways? I was out to get mine my whole life; it was what I was taught was important.

One of the first missions God sent me on was to experience the pain He feels for us. I had arrived in San Antonio, Texas for my son's high school baseball tournament about two hours before the game. I was parked at a convenience store, drinking a cup of coffee and reading my Bible. A man came up to my window and was in a panic. He was trying to tell me something about his wife and his big rig truck, and then he said he did not have enough money to pay his hotel room bill. I asked him to get in my car and have a Coke or Gatorade, and we could figure out what he needed.

When I closed my Bible, I kept my thumb on the page I was reading. He got in the car and started to explain he needed money to pay his room bill. Before he got into the car, I had reached into my wallet and pulled all the cash out and sat it on the console. We shared some scripture, and I told him everything would be all right. He then quoted scripture from The Book of Jeremiah. I asked him how old he was, and when he said forty-one, tears welled up in my eyes. I felt as if this was my father's spirit in the man's body. Why I thought that, I don't know, but I assume it just hit me that this man was the same age as my father when he died. I know my father's spirit was not in this man, but it just seemed such a coincidence that he was the very age my father had been at his death.

The man watched me open my Bible, and to my surprise, my thumb was on the scripture he had quoted. As soon as I asked him how much money he needed, he said, "And the devil is the great deceiver." He grabbed my money, jumped out of my car, and started running. My old self would have chased him down, kicked his butt, and had the police come get him. This time though, all I could do was sit there and cry. I was hurting for him. I knew I could get my wife to send me some more cash, but all I could do was cry for that man as he ran from my car.

After I stopped crying, I started reading again. Then, in a split second, the man climbed back in my car. He asked me some more about Jesus, and I shared with him. Then he said he had to go and thanked me. I never thought about the money. I left there and went over to the game. My son's team was winning by several runs in the fourth, so I left to go over to the grocery store to have Kim wire me some more cash.

While I was waiting there, I sat outside on a park bench, and listened to a song on the speaker system. It was describing how we can't help them all, but God can. I was also watching the people come in and out of the store, and there were women with little children, several of whom were pregnant. I was seeing poverty like I had never seen before, and it was right here in our country. I think mission trips to other countries are great, but why aren't we planning mission trips to our own states and cities?

After getting my money, I went back to the ballpark for the next game. That night I was going to drive home, but as I grew incredibly sleepy at the halfway point. So I stopped at a roadside motel and got a room. The next morning, I woke up early and had some coffee and some fruit. I met a elderly Hispanic man, and we made small talk. I asked him if he lived there. He said no, but it was a very exciting day for him. He was going to get to see his son who he had not seen in quite awhile. His son worked as a ranch foreman, and he was going to get to spend the whole day with him while he worked. It was the first time in my life that I could see the real beauty in family. God showed me that it does not matter where you are or what you are doing; family is wonderful. We should be like that eighty year old man who was about to have the time of his life. In the past, I had always in the past been jealous of those who had a great father-son relationship.

I will never forget the excitement on that man's face and in his voice. I left the hotel and headed back to San Antonio for the last game of the tournament. As I watched my son play, I experienced a joy that was entirely new. When my son was playing, I would usually put an added pressure on myself, hating that he may feel less than successful if he was never able to play pro sports. I admit that I was also hoping he would be the best one on the field, though I kept that sentiment to myself.

I never really wanted any of my boys to play baseball because I only knew it as a game that came easy to me and thought it should be easy for everyone else. I also knew baseball as a business; a very cruel business. People in baseball did not care for you as a person; they cared about what you could do to help the team win.

I would go through many difficult times with my youngest son Andy and high school baseball his senior year. I came to realize that some high school coaches have no clue as to how baseball players need to be nurtured. With my new business of helping high school baseball players try to find baseball scholarships, I had to make some trips to East Texas, and I encountered many different baseball programs and methods.

On one particular trip, I was driving to the Tyler area. It was a Saturday, and I was listening to the radio when something caught my eye; it was a church. It seemed every time I looked up, there was a church. At one point, I started to get a little scared, thinking again that maybe I was going to die. Then I started to ask God what He was trying to tell me.

I had remembered talking to my brother Johnie right after I was released from the hospital.

"Glenn, it sounds to me like you've have been called," he said.

"Johnie, I don't think so." As soon as I said it, I immediately had that pain in my chest again.

"But if that's what God wants, that's what I'll do." The pain went away.

While I was driving and talking to God, I asked Him, "Do you want me to become a preacher?" I pulled my car off the road.

God did not say anything this time. He did not have to because as I looked out my passenger-side window, I noticed I was in the driveway of a Baptist church, and on the other side of the road was a Methodist church. I just sat there and cried as I realized clearly God's call to ministry on my life.

When I got to the destination of the player I was supposed to see later that evening, they asked me over to their ranch. The ranch was owned by a man who had grown up with my middle brother, Roe. In their field, where I had just thrown some batting practice to four high school boys, I was now preaching to them. Glenn Wilson was ministering. What in the world was going on? Three of the boys were not attentive, although one seemed to be listening. The one that was attentive was growing up similar to me: no dad, just a mom.

That night the parents cooked a great meal, and I sat by the fire with the boys and their parents. I noticed that there were five boys there: four baseball players and one boy that played golf, but he was a really bright kid. Every time I would ask the boys a question, the dads would try and answer for them. I noticed how the one dad kept putting the "non-athletic boy" down. I decided that after I asked a question, I would just tell the dad to hold on and let him answer. I could see the mothers noticing what was happening, but the dads were getting frustrated. I realized that is how most of us are; we try to answer for our sons when really we should be listening to them. I am as guilty of it as anyone. God made them just as unique as us.

Later that night, when it was just the men talking, I asked them about their dads. One man broke down crying, saying his dad was an alcoholic and never came to his games. Another dad said his dad would beat him if he had a bad game. The other man never said a word. We had all finished talking, and it was just him and me. He said, "I'm just the son of a carpenter." I knew by that statement he had read the Word. I also knew he was the one who I had been told had done time in prison. He was there that night with his stepson.

The ride home was uneventful, but the ranch I had just left was built exactly the way I had described what I would have someday. I had actually seen that place in my mind many years previous to seeing it in person. The next few trips I had to make were all similar in that I would see so many churches, and my curiosity started to rise. I was still not sure if that was what they meant by feeling called to the ministry. I got even more confused when I started to see cemeteries, more churches, and crosses on the side of the road where someone had died. I was like Gideon in the book of Judges looking for a unmistakable sign.

My next trip was to Kansas to see a college player. While driving through Lufkin, Texas, I got a phone call that a friend of mine was in a hospital in Ft. Worth. So naturally, I cut across East Texas to get to Highway 45. God was still showing me things constantly, many of which reminded me of my family. One of the most interesting things actually happened as I was talking to my wife on the cell phone. She said something about Lance and at the same time she said his name, I was looking at a candy sign from the company Lance.

Then while traveling through the small town of Crockett, Texas, I saw a young person wearing a baseball uniform. I knew he was walking to his ballpark, so I stopped and asked him if he needed a ride. As he got in the car, I noticed he was wearing a Detroit Tigers uniform. I asked him if he knew Jesus. His response was, "Duh." Then when I pulled up to his park, I noticed it was named after Jamie Easterly, a former Major League pitcher. As the young man got out of my car, I saw he was wearing the same number my youngest son Andy had worn in high school.

I headed for the freeway, and upon arriving in Huntsville, there was a hitchhiker. I had never picked up a hitchhiker in my life. This was not even optional now as I pulled over and a man around my age hopped into my truck. He said very little at first. I asked him where he was going, and he said he had work waiting on him in Utah. He told me his name was David Reed. We made small talk, and then he told me he had been working in Florida after Hurricane Katrina. When the work was done, his wife had taken his daughter and moved back to Maine, where they had originally lived. I asked him how he got to Huntsville, and he said he was hitchhiking. I started to share with him about my life-changing experience and my son Lance's drug issues.

This guy knew more about The Bible than anyone I ever met or heard of; he even knew a lot about the lost scrolls. I stopped him on that subject and told him I didn't think I was ready to go there. We drove to Ft. Worth after stopping to get a bite to eat. As we were getting close to Ft. Worth, I remembered that I did not get the name of the hospital. As soon as I remembered that, I saw a cloud in the sky shaped like a cross over the city. I knew to follow it. I did, and sure enough, it was right over the hospital.

I parked the car and told David I might be awhile. I left him the keys in case he needed to go get something. Now why would I leave my car with a complete stranger? I went into the hospital, up the elevator, and right to my friend's floor. His parents, who I had never met, were there. They asked me to not tell him that he had had a heart attack, because it would scare him even more. I said to not worry, that I wouldn't. Then I walked into the ICU. He looked like death.

"How you doing?"

"Not good," he whispered as he could barely talk.

"What about that decision you were trying to make a few years back?" I remembered us talking about accepting Jesus. He had told me a few years prior that he had not made the decision.

"Are you ready to accept Christ?" I asked him.

"Yes," he said. So we prayed the sinner's prayer. He then took his mask off and began to cry and confess sins.

As he was doing this, I glanced at his blood pressure machine. In my mind, I was an expert at reading them because of those heart incidents back in my playing days. As he spoke, his blood pressure came close to being normal.

After he was finished confessing, he asked me something I could not believe. "Will you baptize me?"

Without hesitation, I saw a water bottle on his tray, opened it, and poured some on my hand and his head, as if I had done it a thousand times. "In the name of the Father, the Son, and the Holy Spirit, I baptize thee."

He then started to talk about how much better a pitching coach he was going to be now that he had Christ in his life. After talking with him a little longer, I left the hospital. David and I booked a hotel room and spent the night in Ft. Worth.

We got up the next day and headed for Kansas. I dropped David off on I-40 in Oklahoma and gave him a hundred dollars. We exchanged phone numbers, and that's when God spoke through him to me. He said, "You cannot start your ministry until you make sure that Lance is well and on his way to recovery...Family first." I would get a similar message from a random African-American lady. After hearing my testimony she told me, "Your wife has to be on board before your ministry will start." At that point, I had never told anyone I wanted to preach.

Chapter 11

On one of the trips I made to Mississippi to see my brother, Johnie, he really wanted to show me where our parents grew up. He also wanted me to see the gravesites of our grandparents and great-grandparents. To me this was the best of all my trips. Johnie had become a very private person. He lived on modest means and was afraid I would be embarrassed about how he lived.

He made arrangements for me to stay in a hotel about forty miles from him. So I stayed at the hotel and picked him up that next morning around ten.

We headed over to Monticello first, which was the town where our dad grew up. That evening, after seeing where our dad went to school and visiting the courthouse to see our grandfather's signature on some documents, we met with our dad's best friend from childhood. He told us some funny stories we had not heard about our dad. For some reason, I had never felt a need to know anything about my dad since Johnie and our mom had told me all that I had ever asked. Plus, I did not know the man because he died when I was a kid, but Johnie has missed him ever since he saw him take his last breath.

As we visited with dad's old friend, I asked him if he knew Jesus. He said he did, but he was a Buddhist. Well, that was all it took to compel me to share some things about The Bible with him. That night, in my dad's hometown, his former childhood friend accepted Jesus into his heart.

We got up the next day, and the fun began. First, we met with a man named Wilson, who was a second or third cousin. He took us out to this old sawmill that our grandfather had started in a town that used to be called Wilson Village. We could see old remnants of the saw mill; it was a little eerie, but in a good way.

We went into town, had some lunch, and walked the main street. I stopped at a gift shop that was closed and noticed it was full of Christian items. As I bent down in front of the window, and read a framed picture with the words to "Amazing Grace," I burst into tears. I had never known the second verse.

Twas Grace that taught my heart to fear,
and grace my fears relieved,
how precious did that grace appear,
the hour I first believed

I composed myself, stood up, and pressed my nose to the door window. Out of nowhere, an African American lady opened the door from the inside. She introduced herself and invited us in. She said she was normally closed at that time, but she felt a need to come by the store. I was so excited. I was buying Bibles and books for my family. Then she asked where we were from and what was going on with me.

"What do you mean," I asked.

"I mean what is going on with you?"

So I started to tell her about my experiences. Then a man walked in just as I started to speak.

"Pastor, this is Glenn Wilson, and he was just about to give me his testimony," the lady said.

"I was walking by and felt the presence of the Holy Spirit, and I wanted to tell the boy he has been anointed," the Pastor told her.

"What does that mean?" I asked.

"It means you have God's power, Son." I was taken back, and I mean way back. That was too deep for me at that time. I gave my testimony, and we went on our way, one hundred and sixty dollars lighter. My purchases included the framed picture that actually played "Amazing Grace."

Our next stop was Macomb, where our mom grew up. It was already getting dark, and Johnie wanted to show me the graves, so we bought some flashlights before heading to Macomb. First, Johnie said he had a surprise for me. When we arrived in Macomb, he made me pull around to a high school. I could tell we were pulling up to a baseball field, and the only place to park was behind the right field fence. It seemed appropriate.

As I got out of the car it was dark, and I was watching my steps as I started towards the outfield fence. As I came to some grass I stopped because there was a baseball between my feet.

"Now if Dad is on this field with two gloves, that would be a surprise," I said. I picked up the ball and headed towards the fence, moving closer to Johnie.

"This is where it all started," Johnie said.

"Where all what started?"

"This is where our Mom and Dad first saw each other."

"What?"

"Dad was on the baseball team, and Mom was in the stands."

"Johnie, you never told me Dad played baseball."

"I thought you knew."

I was blown away. I was forty-nine years old, and my dad died when I was six. I played ten years of Major League Baseball and never knew my dad was a baseball player. I knew my mom had been an All-State basketball player in high school. I also knew from my brother that our dad loved baseball, but I never knew he played.

When I got back to Texas, I looked at that ball and could tell it was pretty old and weathered. My youngest son's birthday, 7-10-91, was inscribed in that ball. I still have it to this day.

We left the park and headed to the cemetery. This would be my chance to scare Johnie. It was midnight, and there we were, wandering around a cemetery with flashlights, looking for relative's graves. Since Johnie had heard the story about my experience in the hospital, I had this bright idea that I would lie on one of the graves and start acting like Dad's spirit had entered my body by talking to him in a strange voice.

The joke ended up being on me. He was not fooled, and as I was getting off the grave, I went to pick up the flowers I had knocked over to put them back on the head stone. Then, as I was trying to straighten them, I saw the first name on the headstone was Glenn, spelled like mine. As I moved the light over to see the last name, it was Williams. Wow! I was spooked. Johnie and I laughed for an hour. We went to the other side of the graveyard, and he showed me a lot of our relatives.

The next day we went to an old plantation. It was owned by a family with the last name of Williams. This last name is where we Wilson's came from as my brother had discovered researching our family tree. When we got to the Williams' place, my brother explained that our great-grandfather used to own it. He and his wife are buried there. It was a small cemetery with a small fence around it, on top of a hill that overlooks the entire plantation.

While I was looking at the headstones, Johnie was talking with the new owner. I prayed for their souls, praying that they had known Christ. I noticed some stones outside the fence to the left. I asked what was over here.

"That's where the slaves are buried," the Williams man told me.

"Where are their headstones?"

"They did not give slaves headstones back then," Johnie spoke up.

"How awful." I prayed by interceding and asking forgiveness for my family's sins and for God's favor for the ancestors of the slaves.

When we left, Johnie wanted to show me a house. We drove down about a half mile, and on the left was the house where our Dad was born. The house was big with a wraparound porch that covered the entire front of the house. The gate was locked so we did not walk up to the house. We went down the road a little further and took a left that was running parallel with the property. Johnie was trying to point something else out as were going up a small hill. That was when I noticed a small white church on the right. I looked at the clock, it was seven on a Wednesday night, and I said we were going to church.

I pulled in the parking lot, grabbed my Bible, and we entered the building. To this day, I am not sure if they were having Bible study or a church service. When we sat down, the man speaking at the front had no front teeth. Everyone in the church was African American. While the man was speaking to the congregation, I was reading in my Bible. I knew something was going to happen but was not sure what God had in mind. The preacher and the rest of the congregation turned and looked at us. The preacher said, "Welcome brothers. Is there anything you would like to add?" Well, that was all it took for me to realize what God wanted us to do.

God stood me up, and I started reading my Bible out loud. Soon I was preaching and wound up at the front of the church. When I finished, I said, "Now, let's pass the offering plate." I grabbed the offering plate and took it to the first seat on each row, until all rows were covered. I then took it back to the front and handed it to the little old lady to the side. As she took it from me, she pulled my arm down so she could whisper something in my ear.

"God bless you child; you know you've been anointed."

"Yes ma'am, I keep hearing that." I still did not know what it meant.

We stood outside visiting with some of the congregation, and I overheard Johnie saying he was real sorry that our ancestors had owned their ancestors. When Johnie and I got back to my car, he said something that I will treasure more than anything he has ever said to me. "Glenn, I am so proud of you. I have never known you as a man, only as a kid. That sermon was great."

"Well it wasn't me. I do not even know what I said."

"I knew when we walked in you were going to preach."

I like how God will just wing it. That was how I had always been. I was never afraid to speak in public and had even spoken at my mother's funeral. That was my first time to preach in a church. How about that? What made it more special was it was in-between my mom and dad's hometowns. God loves to wow me.

The next day I would have to say goodbye to Johnie and head back to Texas. I never told him this, but I cried for about twenty miles because I already missed him. I was able to go back and get him two more times: once to bring him to one of Andy's high school football playoff games, and once to take him to the airport so he could fly to Vegas and see his son. I enjoyed those times with him more than any other times in our lives. He and I are closer now than ever before, and he told me that the way he serves the Lord is by prayer.

After the visitation of the Holy Spirit and my trip to Mississippi, I had returned home, while still living in a spiritual world. This is not like how we usually talk about the spiritual; this was different. I only had eyes and ears for God. I could communicate perfectly, but I was only seeing what God wanted me to see. I once told my wife that it was like living in Heaven while here on earth.

I would drive with my Bible in the car. When I was at a red light or traffic was stopped, I would see a license plate. I would look at the letters and numbers and then open my Bible to what was on the plate. If I saw a plate with JJH 319, I would open The Bible to John chapter 3 verse 19. It would speak directly to my heart.

Since I was going to church all the time and reading my Bible, my youngest son, Andy, was confused by me. He said he wanted his old dad back. I told him that man had died. It took three months, but Andy began to love the man I had become. He used to call me his old man, but now he calls me Pops. Our relationship continued to grow closer and closer as the days passed by.

I once went to Pasadena to look at a high school player that had called me about helping him find a scholarship. When I got in my car, I remembered I left the directions in the house. I remember thinking that I didn't need them. I knew where Pasadena was and God would help me find the field at the right time.

We headed out and as I was coming into the area, I asked a family in their front yard where the stadium was. When I got there, it was the wrong stadium, but there was a young man hitting in the cage at that field. I offered him some pointers, and he gave me directions to the correct field. At that field, I walked over to the home side and sat down on the front row. As I was sitting there, an older lady was sitting to my left. She turned out to be one of my mother's friends that had children the same age as my brothers and me.

Later I visited with the player I was there to see and knew that his abilities were not college material, but I told him to call me if he wanted some help. He did not call, thank goodness.

Another time I was driving home from visiting the family of a player who had good college potential when I had a blow out on the toll road. I was not mad or worried. I climbed out of my car, and in five minutes a wrecker truck pulled up. A young man jumped out and explained the toll road authority had just started a new program of helping any and all motorist to stay on the road to keep traffic moving.

"When did this start?" I asked him.

"Today."

I just started laughing and praising God.

After he jacked up my car, he could not get the lug nuts to turn. I reached in my car for my Bible, and then went to my trunk. I grabbed a baseball bat and came to the tire. I tried hitting the lug wrench while it was on the lug nuts, but nothing happened. So the tow driver had to call someone to come help us. I went to the trunk and started to read my Bible. For some reason, I started to pray and quote some scripture. I remembered that all things are possible with God. I asked God to help me get the tire off. When my hand touched the tire wrench, it just turned with ease.

"How did you do that?" yelled the man. I looked at him and showed him that my *Bible* was in my left hand.

"All things are possible with God."

"You're right," he said while shaking his head. "You know, I thought we were going to have to tow your car. There was no way those lug nuts were coming off when I tried. That was a miracle."

I just laughed and pointed at the sky.

"God is good."

As I was traveling to different towns and baseball games, I was still noticing churches and cemeteries. This started to really make me think. Was I being told by God that I was going to die soon, or was the devil messing with me again?

During this seven-month period, I was telling people my story, and it got different responses from different people. There would be some that God would use to give me answers. One man told me that I would have died if it had not been for God's intervention.

One time I was getting a brake job done on my truck. The worker was taking a break, and I asked him what his favorite verse in the Bible was. He said Galatians 2:20. I picked up my Bible and read it. It said, "I have been crucified with Christ; and it is no longer I who live, but Christ lives in me; and the life which I now live in the flesh I live by faith in the Son of God, who loved me and gave Himself up for me." I was stunned. It was the perfect description of my experience and the resulting transformation. Christ was truly living inside of me for one reason and one reason only: God had met me in my search for meaning and truth, and I had run to Him. I had finally, at the age of 49, surrendered all.

I needed answers. It was obvious to me after my trip to Mississippi that God had anointed me, so I started calling ministers. I wanted to know what anointed meant and what was happening to me. I knew God was involved, but it was deeper than I could understand on my own. I tried to get a meeting with the head pastor at the mega-church where I was led before my hospital stay, but he was just too busy. When working for a growing mega-church, the head pastor can be consumed with more important issues. I was just thankful they were open on a Monday. I met many people that were friends with him who said they would call him so we could all do lunch. That never happened, so I accepted that God did not want us to sit down together until the timing was right.

I called more pastors and most of them were not available to sit down with me. I knew I had a personal relationship with our Father, but I really wanted to connect with other men who were living out the calling which God had placed on my life. I continued to watch a few ministers on TV. My favorites were Creflo Dollar, Joyce Meyer, and Dr. Ed Young. I watched the *700 Club* consistently as well.

I had an experience watching the Christian channel back in 1981. I had just been called up to Evansville, the Tigers' triple A team, from Double A Birmingham. I had gotten in around ten o'clock. Pat Robertson was on the 700 club talking about witnessing. Before I climbed into bed, I hit my knees and prayed. "God, tomorrow give me someone to witness to, and please don't let me forget this prayer."

The next morning, I asked the lady at the front desk where the mall was located. That is what most players did back in those days: went to malls, had lunch, and looked at things to buy. She told me the mall was about a thirty-minute drive and I could get a taxi out front. So I headed out.

When I got in the car, the taxi driver started telling me every problem he had going on in his life. I was in a good mood since I would be playing my first Triple A game that night. Then it hit me, and I remembered my prayer. I was thinking that could be my chance to witness. I had not witnessed to anyone since high school, right after I had been saved. That only lasted two weeks because I was losing friends with my shove-it-down-your-throat approach. I was going to be really cautious this time.

When the man finished telling me about how he and his wife were at their wit's end, I calmly said, "I don't want you to think I am some kind of Jesus freak, but have you ever tried God?"

"Yeah, we tried going to church, but that didn't work either."

"No, I mean do you have a personal relationship with Jesus?"

"No."

So I started to tell him how when I accepted Christ, He started doing all these things for me. He allowed me to get drafted in baseball and to make good money playing a kids' game for a living. I went on and on. I told him if he wanted to accept Jesus, I would pray with him. He said no thanks, but that he would think about it. I felt so dejected, like I did not say the right words. We arrived at the mall, and I got out and went to pay my fare.

"I'm sorry," I said, "I never even asked you your name."

He turned his head and looked at me with his crystal blue eyes.

"I'm Glenn Wilson," he said.

I was frozen.

"No. Really?"

He quickly said, "I gotta go," and drove off. I started to get teary-eyed as I realized this was not about me witnessing. This was about God reminding me that He was still with me. Even though I was not acting like a Christian, or being obedient, or even reading His Word, He was still with me. I was dumb-founded the rest of the day. I had never met anyone with the same name as me. God had commanded my attention, but it would be short lived again.

There was another time God used me in spite of my disobedience. It was in St Louis back in June of 1984. Phillies' Public Relations director, Vince Nauss, traveled with our team for the away games. Vince was one of the nicest people you could ever meet. Many times on road trips we would eat together, watch TV, talk, and hang out. I often subjected Vince to my love of John Wayne movies. One night we were watching TV after a game when he started to share some things about his family that with me that were personal. I really did not know what to say.

"Have you given it to God?" I asked.

"I have no idea how to do that."

Vince got up to leave the room, and out of nowhere I knew I had to ask him a question. "Vince, are you absolutely certain you'd go to Heaven if you die in your sleep tonight?"

Vince turned around and answered me, "Yeah, I am pretty sure I would go to Heaven. You know I'm a good person and if God were to place the good and bad things on a scale, the good would definitely win out."

As Vince sat back down, I grabbed the Gideon Bible from the drawer and flipped to Ephesians 2:8-9 which says, "For by grace you have been saved through faith; and that not of yourselves, it is the gift of God; not as a result of works, so that no one may boast."

I then encouraged Vince to consider what God's Word said and if he believed salvation was a gift instead of something to be earned. I also encouraged him to pray and acknowledge that he was trusting in Jesus' payment on the cross for his salvation since there was nothing else that he could do on his own. That night Vince believed what I said, and more importantly, he believed what the Bible said. He was saved that very night as we prayed together. From that day forward Vince was different because he had caught fire for Christ.

I have no idea why he would believe me. I was not an example for Christ. I was living life for myself, my family and the lusts of the flesh. Many years later, after I was out of baseball, I read his testimony in a Christian baseball magazine, and recognized my name. I remember thinking that I was going to Heaven since I saved him and he was now president of Major League Baseball chapel, saving souls all around baseball. I was good to go.

First of all, I did not save him; Jesus did. I was just the messenger boy. In my old way of thinking, I had done it. What I think is so awesome is that even though I was not walking with Christ, He was still able to use me. He could have used John Denney, because John was walking with Christ, but he chose to use me.

I struggled with going to chapel as a player because when you drank until two in the morning after a game and then had a Sunday day game, the last thing I wanted to do was go to chapel. There were times I wanted to attend, but I struggled with two things. One was I knew I would be a hypocrite. The second was that solemn feeling I used to get after church when I was little. I did not think I could play a Major League Baseball game with a soft heart and didn't think it would be good if a player who had just attended chapel subsequently was cursing an umpire or checking out some girl with in a bikini top in the stands. That was not Christ-like.

I guess you could say I loved baseball games more than I loved Christ. I was saved, and as far as I knew, that was all that mattered. I could commit any sin, ask for forgiveness, and then be ok. While I was a baseball player, I committed many sins. There was temptation everywhere in the hotel bars, at the malls, and especially on the road. I tried a little of the whole buffet. I am not proud of it, and it is not easy to admit. I thought I was going to heaven, because I had accepted Jesus, but my actions showed I didn't really love Him. I thought you could do what you wanted and that obedience to Christ did not matter. I was making a mockery of His grace.

After all, I was named an All Star; I thought I was better than people because I had money, fame, and fortune. It turns out what I really had was pride, pride, and more pride. I had people that I paid to pay my bills. I was falling into a trap of self-love and pride. I had a charity golf tournament named after me, and I did not even care where the money was going. Though for some reason, I would not go to the hospital to have my picture taken when we were giving the charity check; I guess deep down I knew my heart was not in the right place.

I cannot count how many guilty nights I had, knowing I had done something wrong, but would do it again. I remember praying many nights, "God, please help me stop this foolishness." I was creating my own hell. I could not see how to be a true Christian while playing a professional sport. They just did not go together. How wrong I was. I have wondered many times how could I be so ignorant?

I was afraid of dying young like my dad. I knew about Hell and Heaven. I thought I was basically a good person who believed in Jesus, so if God loved me, He would forgive me. I did not know God's wrath and how jealous He is for His own glory. I was living for my glory instead of living as a proclaimer of His greatness. I had made a public commitment but proved by the way I was living that it was a lie. I had lied to God. There is no eternal salvation for someone that lies to God. I had said I knew him, but in my heart I knew that was a lie. I figure I would have been one of those Jesus talked about in Matthew 7, where the person stands before God and claims they know him and list all the things they did in His name, but He looks at them and says He never knew them. I believed in Him, but until that transformation after my career, I had not given myself completely to Him.

Chapter 12

I believe now that you must accept Jesus as Lord, ask for His forgiveness of sins, and give your complete heart to God to allow Him to do what He wants in and through you. A relationship with God is more than just believing He is real; even the demons believe this and shudder. It is abandoning your life and pursuit of your own glory to live for His glory.

One of the most important ways to build intimacy with God is to read His Word. It is a road map to Heaven. We must live it out in authenticity as ambassadors for Christ. God tells us in 2 Corinthians 5:17 that when we come to know Him, we become a new creation. In 5:20 He tells us that the way we live out what He has done in us allows Him to plead through our lives that others come to know Him. God makes all things work together for the good of those who love Him; I truly believe this. God takes all things and makes them work for His purposes. We will know each other by our fruits: the fruits of the spirit. When we truly belong to Him, the things that come out of our lives will reflect Him. I spent a lot of my life claiming to know Him while exhibiting no fruit.

When I was engulfed in the Holy Spirit, my wife and son said I was repeating the words "Love, Faith, Trust." I do not remember that, but I can only tell you that from the first night of my visitation from The Holy Spirit, I knew I was going to die. I thought I was going to die physically, but I realize now I was going to die to my old self. This experience has changed me, and my family witnessed it. It changed my relationship with Kim and my boys dramatically. God's voice that used to seem so distant now seems so clear; I know He is speaking to me.

I once was blind, but now I see. God's grace is so amazing. Why would He care about me? I made him look bad by my actions towards so many people. I made myself look bad. I made Jesus, who lives inside me, look bad, yet He did not give up on me. The moment I accepted Christ, He came into my heart and took up residence. I would deny Him many times, just as the disciples would. Why are we like that?

I went in search of God and He showed up. He showed me love and true faith. Now He expects me to trust Him. I do Father, I really, really do. I am still tempted; the devil tries to attack me in different areas. Sometimes the enemy gets to me, but when I start to look to Jesus for strength, He is always there.

I started writing this book many years before I surrendered all to Christ. I was transformed by an experience that to some will seem unbelievable, while others will try to explain it away as some painkiller withdrawal episode. I used to be the same way when I heard of testimonies like this that I could not understand. In fact, I did not believe them, but then again, I had not read God's Word.

I continue to read God's Word daily and try to meditate on it. There have been many times where I find myself in search of the meaning of my calling. Why have I been called to preach? Why me? What is God's will for my life now? I thought I had a couple of jobs, but I know God shut them down, mainly so I could write this book.

I really hope this book helps people realize one thing. God is real, and He is not far off. It is so easy for us to only think of God on Sundays, but he is the God of every day, every hour and every minute.

I also hope this book helps you if you are hooked on painkillers. If you're trying to quit, you can when you allow God to come in and heal you. Do not be ashamed and do not try to do it alone. Seek out a drug rehab center that focuses on Christ. My son Lance was in a sentenced rehab and is now doing great through the healing of God. I hear him sounding like a preacher now, too. I believe all addictions are beatable if you involve God.

I know how strange this story may sound for many of you reading this book. So I would like to take this time to encourage you to read Jeremiah 17:7. God is real. Jesus is the Son of God. There is a real Heaven and a Hell. I was chosen to see them both. When I did, the gates of Heaven were closed, and Hell had no gate in sight. I will forever be changed by that awesome experience. I am not special, nor will I ever be perfect.

I am a sinner that was wandering in the dark for a long time. If I had died on February 12, 2008, even though

I believed in Jesus, I do not believe I would have gone to Heaven because I did not have a relationship with Him at that time. I pray that when I stand before the Judgment Seat, God will say "Well done my good and faithful servant," as He welcomes me with open arms. Jesus will say to the Father on my behalf, "I died for this man's sins, and I paid his price in full."

The Bible says, "Do not be conformed to this world, but transformed by the renewing of your mind." Although some thought I lost my mind for awhile, I believe during those awesome seven months God was transforming my mind to think like those who belong to Him and not like the fleshly man I once was. I am still very hungry to know more about God's Word and more importantly, I am still passionate about sharing the Good News.

Think about this if you would: the truth is that someday we all are going to die. If The Bible is right, which I believe it is, then every knee will bow and all those who trusted in Jesus and accepted Him as Lord and Savior will enter into His Kingdom. Those that do not trust in Him will go to a real place called Hell.

God knows your heart. If you living life for yourself, never surrendering to Him, and sinning with no thought of remorse, think again about what being His child really means. Give him your life; you have a chance, right now, to know where you will spend eternity.

You must ask Jesus to come into your heart and make Him the Lord of your life. You must ask Him to forgive you of your sins, and then repent and renounce those things in your life that do not bring Him glory. Repent means "to turn away from." Part of giving Him your heart is standing for the truth and turning away from the junk that steals our affection for Him. I would suggest that you start reading The Bible, because all the answers on how to live your life for Christ are in there.

Living God's way will not be easy, but have you ever heard of anything worth having that was easy? I cannot express the importance of living your life for the one and only person that died for you. He is the way, the truth, and the life. This world we live in seems to be on its way to destruction, but Christ brings life. When your time on Earth is done, or God decides it is time to return, what will be your eternal destination?

To any young person who reads this and is full of ambition and drive, knowing you are on your way to the Big Leagues, I can personally say that if you think for one minute that you will have time later to live for Christ, think again. You might be killed in a car wreck today or develop a brain tumor tomorrow. Why would anyone put off the most important decision of their life when it comes to where eternity will be spent?

I know how hard life can be. I lost my dad at six. I lost my mom at thirty. I have lived the Big League life with all its temptations, and was sucked in to the glitz and glamour. I thought I had it all: fame, fortune, and people wanting my autograph. I was hanging out with celebrities of all professions. I even met a president, but I had forgotten about the one person that died for me so I could spend eternity with Him, my mother and my father.

My dad was the man I never got to play catch with, but I can only imagine what it is going to be like when I get to meet my heavenly Father and then my earthly father. If my earthly dad says, "Hey, son, I sure am proud of you," then those words will be echoing through Heaven, but more than that I want to live a life that makes sure my heavenly Father says, "Welcome son, job well done."

So let me ask you one question right now. Do you know where you are going after this life? You can be certain by accepting Jesus and giving Him your life. You may be saying right now, "There is no way God will accept me; I have been an awful person." God sent His Son for everyone. We all mess up and fall short of His mercy and love.

I was a bad guy. I thought that Sparky, Leyland, and Bill Wood were all out to get me, but the truth is I was selfish.

I thought my college coach was wrong for what he put me through, but I was wrong. All that I went through was a part of God's plan to bring me into a personal relationship with Him. I thought my agents were the bad guys, and when I would get traded, I was ticked at the people that traded me. I was wrong for thinking that way. I wish I could go back and apologize to all those people, but for now I can only do it through this book. I pray they will forgive me.

Now I believe that if you want to be a Big Leaguer, you can be a true Christian at the same time. I want to apologize to all the managers, coaches, and teammates that I encountered when playing baseball for being an "I" person. I always made it about me and sometimes took things out on you when my pride was injured. To the people who were closest to me, my wife and family, I am sorry for being a phony Christian and not living as an example of Christ in front of you. To my brothers, I am sorry for deserting you. This also applies to the Hendricks Brothers, too. I am sorry for giving up on you and walking out.

To the guys I managed, I should have taken the time to read The Bible during those four years we were together. I thought I was functioning normally, but I was not the man that God needed me to be as an example for you young men.

Young athletes, don't wait to make this decision about Jesus; please make it now. I promise that if you do, you can hold your head up high while you are chasing your dream. There will come a time when your playing days are over and you will have to do something else with your time and passions. I trust you to consider that while you are still in school. I did not prepare for it, but God still had enough grace for me to be able to share with you what not to do and to tell you what to do.

If you think you are reading this by coincidence, you are sadly mistaken. God knows you and your heart, and He is using these words, this very minute, to share with you the most important play of your life. This is one play where you can't afford to make an error.

Like the song says, "Softly and tenderly Jesus is calling, calling for you and for me." What are you waiting for? Go get a Bible and read John 3:16. You want real power? Continue to read His Word on a daily basis. Live in His supernatural Spirit, and you will see real power. The older I get and the more I read, the more I see how deceived I was in my past. This world will pass away, but those that believe will not be disappointed. Those that do not believe will be on a hot streak forever.

The normal thing to think is, "Oh, here is another story of a big time athlete that went broke, got on drugs, and found God." Yeah, you're right, except for the part about being a big time athlete. I was average at best, but for some reason you bought this book and are reading it right now. You think that is a coincidence? You might be a Major League player right now and going through the same struggles I did about going to chapel and feeling that those Christians are a bunch of weaklings. They're not, and you're not as good as you think you are; it is God that supplies the power and you are just one of his instruments.

If you are a current player and think that being a nice guy does not matter, think again. Those sports writers around you have a vote for the Hall of Fame. Someday, you will be out of the game, and you will look back at your career and be able to say, "Thank God I accepted Jesus." Or like me, you will have to say, "Why did I not give God everything?"

Most of the people that I was around during my playing days will probably say that Glenn Wilson was a nice guy. I know they won't say Glenn Wilson was a strong Christian man. I was completely into myself and what I could get. I encourage you to not make the same mistake.

I also encourage you to watch out for the preachers that only want to tell you the good parts of The Bible. They have their reward also, and there are many televangelists that need to check themselves. I believe in being positive, but stop sugarcoating the Word. God is just and He knows our hearts and our motives. Everything done in the dark will be brought to the light.

Today, as for me, I am a licensed minister that happened to be a baseball player. Imagine that! I am nothing but a child of God that is thankful for His grace! I will trust in Jesus. During the 1985 All-star game, with the bases loaded, I struck out with a three and two count. Like that matters. Well, the count right now is three and two, and the bases are loaded. What will be your outcome? Will they say, "he was a nice guy," or will they say, "I know he's in Heaven"?

God Bless you. I pray you will step up to the plate and take a swing for Jesus. He is waiting, and through the power of His Spirit you can change. If you have already accepted Christ, then tell someone else about God's grace, read God's Word daily, and rely on the power of the Holy Spirit to bring it to life. Live powerfully for Him as the same power that raised Christ from the dead lives in you. Christianity is not about our words, but the power of the Spirit working through us. Submit to His power!

I continue to see how God works things out when we can't see how it is possible. We should walk by faith and not by sight. Faith is the hope of things not yet seen. I have not seen God or His Son Jesus, but I know He is real and that He is here. He is nearer to you than you think, and He desires intimacy with you.

You may be wondering, "What do I do next?" I have come to learn that God has the plan. I have not heard from Him what is next for me, but I will tell you this; I knew I would be a pro athlete...I knew it sitting at my dad's funeral. I even knew when Brother Martin tapped my mother on the shoulder the day my dad died that he was gone, but I never could have foreseen the calling God has on my life to be a preacher and writer for His glory. It is a testament to the fact if God can use me, He can use you. Do not miss your chance to impact the only game that truly matters beyond the years of your time here on Earth. Surrendering to Christ...It was my most important play. Life is best lived with our true home in mind; the destination we live for is to cross home plate. Early in my life I ran outside of the baselines and lived for myself, today I am rounding third and heading for home. Paul said it best in Philippians 1:21, *"For me to live is Christ and to die is gain."*

I do not know how many days I have left here on Earth, but as I head home, I live with this mindset: If I am able to live another second, another hour, or another day, it will be about Christ and for Christ. If I die, and cross the home plate of life, I will be in the very presence of Christ. I am finally playing a game that I cannot lose because I am sealed by His power.

By the way, Lance never went through any drug withdraws. He is doing great working for his uncle, Carey Poarch Sr., who God has used to be a blessing not only to Lance, but many others as well. Glenn Jr., Lance, Andy and Kim witnessed their dad and husband go through a life changing experience in which they had every reason to think I was crazy and disown me, but they didn't. As a matter of fact, Glenn Jr. stayed three nights with me in the hospital, and I can never say thank you enough, my son. To Kim, thank you for putting up with me while I lived life in my old wine skin. I know I have not made your life an easy one. You have always been the Angel I saw in that dream. To Lance, I am so proud of you for fighting your demons with courage and strength. Then to Andy, I know that God has His plan for your life, and I know you went through a lot having a brother and father hooked on pills. Well, we are clean now, and thanks for continuing to love us.

I end this book with this passage. I shall boast in my weaknesses for when I am weak, then I am strong.

Bibliography

Fimrite, R. (1990, April 16). You Can't Keep a Good Man Down. *Sports Illustrated.*

Lidz, F. (1989, May 29). This Job's a Gas. *Sports Illustrated.*

Nauss, Vince. "Headed Home Interview." E-mail interview. 8 Aug. 2011.

Baseball-Reference.com - Major League Baseball Statistics and History. Web. 15 Oct. 2011. <http://www.baseballreference.com>.

"DVD VIDEO RECORDER Movie1 Chapter1 - YouTube." *YouTube.* Web. 23 Jan. 2012. <http://www.youtube.com/watch?v=0eL9GoOpE3I>.

"VID-20110913-00003 - YouTube." *YouTube.* Web. 23 Oct. 2011. <http://youtu.be/CqvrUaUEHkw>.

McAlary, Mike. "San Diego Paradise Is A Swing & A Myth - New York Daily News." *Featured Articles From The New York Daily News.* New York Daily News, 16 Oct. 1998. Web. 14 Nov. 2011. http://articles.nydailynews.com/1998-10-16/news/18089817_1_yankee-stadium-brooklyn-navy-yard-padre-third-baseman

Lajoie, Bill. "Chapter 8: "You Get That Guy and We'll Win the World Series!"" *Character Is Not a Statistic: The Legacy and Wisdom of Baseball's Godfather Scout Bill Lajoie.* By Anupam Sinha. [S.l.]: Xlibris, 2010. Print.

Picture Index